Fundamentals of Business

Fundamentals of Business

(WHAT I HAVE LEARNED)

Michael D Lacey

Fundamentals of Business
Copyright © 2015 by Michael D. Lacey

All rights reserved. No part of this book may be reproduced or transmitted in any form or by any means without written permission from the author.

ISBN13: 9781505859591
ISBN-10: 150585959X
Library of Congress Control Number: 2015901983
CreateSpace Independent Publishing Platform
North Charleston, South Carolina

Acknowledgments

This is book was made possible by the many people I have had the pleasure of working with over the years. I have learned a lot from each of them. Too numerous to list here, I thank them all for their many contributions to my own success. Where possible I have tried to give specific credit as appropriate. I apologize if I have inadvertently omitted credit where credit was due.

I thank my wife for all of her support and for her counsel, which has been very helpful to me over the years. She has great insights, and I have benefitted from taking advantage of her perspectives.

Preface

I have been fortunate enough to have learned what is essential to succeed in business. This knowledge has come over more than four decades in the business world, at both very small and very large companies. In this book I have included the fundamental knowledge for building and operating a successful company.

This not a grand treatise on business. It is, rather, a catalogue of accumulated knowledge and experience. As such, it is broken down into easily understandable chapters. Each chapter is intended, as much as possible, to contain only the fundamentals of the covered subject. By necessity, some chapters will refer to information contained in another chapter.

I make no claim that any thoughts in this book are original to me. I have learned everything included here from others, but I cannot categorically acknowledge what information came from whom. I have included sources whenever I knew the specific source and apologize to anyone who should have been credited, but was not. I do very much appreciate each and every person who helped advance my knowledge of business throughout my career.

Every subject here is treated from the ground level—you can find a great deal more information on each in the published literature. Concepts will be discussed in more than one chapter, when necessary, to properly cover a subject. But there is not enough space here to cover everything there is to know about each subject.

Treat this book as a primer to business success. This is a starting point, not an ending point. As with all things in business, it is the beginning of a process that never terminates. Understanding this will serve you well as you read through the following pages.

Table of Contents

Introduction xv

General Management Responsibilities 1
    People 1
    Credit/Collections 2
    Common Problems 3
    Customer-Centric Focus 4
    Money Myths 5

Business Structures 7
    Types of Business Structures 7

Reading and Understanding Financial Statements 9
    Standard Business Terminology 9
        Measures of Business Operations 11
        Liquidity Measures: Current ratio, quick ratio, acid test 11
        Debt Ratios: Debt to assets, debt to equity 12
        Operations: ADRO, ADPO, Asset turnover, break-even point 12
    The Income Statement 13
    The Balance Sheet 17
        Assets 19
        Liabilities 19
        Equity 19
    Analysis of Financial Statements 20

Balance Sheet Analysis	21
Liquidity Measures	21
Leverage	23
Income Statement Analysis	24
Additional Ratios	26
Understanding Cash Flow	29
Calculating Cash Flow	31
The Cash-Flow Statement	31
How to Effectively Manage Working Capital	35
Effective Collection Methods	39
Understanding Insurance	47
A Guide to Planning	51
Why Planning Is Critical	51
Planning Can Be Difficult	52
What Is a Business Plan?	53
Elements of a Business Plan	54
Products and Services	54
Sales and Marketing	55
Financial Management	56
Goal Setting	56
Goal-Setting Template	58
Personal Goals Template	60
Business Goals Template	61
The Budgeting Process	63
The Fundamentals of Budgeting	64
Reaching the Goal	66
Trends	68
Bottom Line	68

Forecasting Sales.. 73
   Realism 74
   Revenue Categories... 76
   Sales-Influencing Factors... 76
      Internal Factors 76
      External Factors... 77
   Gross Margin Percentages 77

   Conclusions.. 79

Marketing Your Company.. 81
   Company Analysis.. 82
   Customer Analysis.. 83
   Competition 85
   Pricing Structure 86
   Promotion and Image 89
   Opportunities.. 91
   Threats... 92
   Basic Marketing Categories 95
   Marketing Goals.. 100
   Strategic Marketing Plan... 102
   Have a Customer-Centric Focus.................................... 107
   Product Introductions... 113

Effective Methods for Managing People 115
   Compensation 116
   Benefits 116
   Interviewing the Candidate 117
   Maintaining Good Employee Relations............................ 119
   Performance Reviews.. 120
   Bonuses and Compensation Increases............................. 129
   Handling Employee Discipline 131
   The Importance of Documentation 133

    Employment Law.. 134
    Culture of Inclusion 135

The Importance of Communication 137
    Initiating Action.. 138
    Establishing a Relationship... 139
    Changing Attitudes and Opinions................................... 140
    Communicating with Customers.................................... 141
    General Communication Guidelines 142
    Some general guidelines:.. 143

Conflict Resolution 145

Leadership Principles... 153
    Recruiting People: Some General Guidelines........................ 154
    Managing People: Some General Guidelines........................ 156
        Involvement 161
        Empowerment 162
        Resistance 163
    Delegation of Tasks... 166
    Managing Yourself.. 168
        Time Management... 169
        Leadership Analysis 173
        Clarity... 175
        Coaching 176
        Perspective.. 177
        Responsibility 178
    Power and Authority 179
    Ways to Improve Your Leadership Skills 182
    Conclusion.. 186

Putting it all Together 189

    Misconceptions 189
    Truths.. 191
    Core Concept 193
    Focus 197
    Entrepreneurship... 203

Index... 207

Introduction

This book presents the basic knowledge required to be successful in business—any business. I have written it from the vantage point of management. It is appropriate to any level of management. Whether you are the company president, a business unit leader, a department leader, or just plan to move into management, the information detailed here should be very relevant to you.

We will start with brief descriptions of some general management responsibilities and then move into more detailed discussions of each topic in later chapters. The management of people, money, and credit are central to business success. Making sure your company has a focus on your customer is essential to long-term growth. We will briefly discuss all of these topics in chapter one.

I hope you can use this book as a guide to help you develop your own methods to improve your business. Please take the information contained here and use it as a starting point. If you understand the basics, you can then use that knowledge to plan and cultivate an environment of success in your business.

General Management Responsibilities

People

The people who succeed in business not only know more than others about what they are doing, they also know how to plan for success and how to manage people, and they realize that they must never stop learning. For example, being a fantastic electrician does not mean you know how to run an electrical contracting company. The expertise necessary for business success is acquired through a combination of study, both formal and informal, and on-the-job experience. This is a knowledge-based proposition—not a proposition based on how hard you work or how much you want to succeed.

To be effective, you must be able to influence key people to get the results you planned for within the cost and time limits allowed. One of the secrets of business success is deciding what items you must control and what items you allow other members of your team to control. Even in a small company, you should not try to be all things to all people. You should keep close control of people, products, money, and any other resources that are significant to keeping the operation pointed toward profitability. Then you must learn and execute effective delegation methods.

Use compensation as a tool to help you achieve the goals of the company. Reward quality work, as this will pay big dividends for the company in the long run. Whereas bonuses reward people for past performance, increases in compensation are an incentive for future performance. So, bonuses are a much desired "pat on the back." Do not underestimate the value of recognizing past performance, both verbally and monetarily. But increases in regular compensation incentivize people to reach even higher levels of productivity. Bonuses are backward looking whereas pay increases are forward looking.

Be systematic in how you apply increases in compensation as well as bonuses. It is important to explain to all of the senior members of your management team how bonuses and compensation adjustments work. Your management team must then pass this information along to members of their teams.

Credit/Collections

A successful manager knows both how much credit he can afford to extend over any period and how much he has already extended. Grant credit willingly, but keep it systematic. Insist on a written credit application and make sure that it contains a promise to pay according to the credit terms you have established.

Invoice customers on time, and be certain to include on the invoice the date of purchase, item(s) purchased, purchase price, and extended amounts. Monthly statements are equally important. These should also show your customer any overdue balance and how long it has been overdue. Statements should be sent out as soon after the close of the month as possible. Keep current statements separate from statements that are past due. Past due statements have balances that are thirty, sixty or ninety days or more past due. Highlight the overdue amounts on the statements.

Not every account will pay promptly. Keep in mind that a slow-paying customer can still be profitable, especially if that customer buys large amounts of high margin items. The danger is in letting such a customer get beyond his or her ability to pay. Set up a system for collecting from late and slow-paying accounts, but bear in mind that in reminding them to pay up, your objective is to get your money without losing their business. (Refer to the section "Effective Collection Methods" for more information.)

Common Problems

Most major business problems fall into to one of the following five categories:

- Cash management
- Internal control systems
- Cost controls
- Management strategies
- Managing people

There can be weaknesses in any area of the above categories. Early diagnosis and correction of these problems can prevent future major headaches in the future. Of the five areas of business problems, cash management is probably the one area where business managers most often need help. Be diligent about your cash management system. Failure to manage cash properly can render the remaining four categories moot. We will deal with this issue in detail in the section on "Cash Flow."

Some key indicators that show which areas may need attention are:

- Loss of customers
- Loss of key employees
- Reduction in gross margins
- Failure to meet budgets and forecasts
- Consistent cash-flow problems
- Consistent accounts receivable problems
- Consistent quality problems

Although this is by no means a comprehensive list, when one or more of these warning signals are spotted it is time to launch a detailed analysis and diagnosis of how the problem occurred and how it may be corrected. One of the most fundamental tools for detailed problem analysis is the SWOT (strengths, weaknesses, opportunities, threats) analysis. This analysis allows you to identify problems and devise corrective measures. We will deal with the SWOT analysis in greater detail in the marketing section, although this analysis can be used for many of the problems a company faces. Each of the above indicators will be covered in an upcoming chapter.

However, nothing is more critical to long-term success than maintaining a customer-centric focus for the company.

Customer-Centric Focus

Deliver the best product or service possible and do everything you can to ensure that your customers are satisfied. This is the creed by which business owners everywhere must live, though upholding it is a constant challenge. Customers are the foundation of all business, so it is absolutely essential to do everything reasonable to please them. Note that I said to do "everything reasonable" not "everything possible." Your strong desire to keep happy your customers happy will sometimes conflict with unrealistic demands made by some customers. Make sure your policies reflect the importance of happy customers, but be willing to recognize when a customer is making an unreasonable demand. When that happens be comfortable about saying, "I'm sorry, but we just cannot do that."

To succeed in business you can't just be "as good as" the next guy. You must be demonstrably better and be able to prove it. Your team should constantly discuss ways you can improve your business. Remember, if you work just for the money, you'll never make it; but if you always put the customer first, you will dramatically improve your chances for success. We will cover the details of being focused on the customer in the "Marketing" section.

Finally, in terms of general responsibilities, the myths surrounding money can be a real problem. So, let's immediately deal with some of those myths.

Money Myths

Myth 1: "If only we had more money coming in, everything would be great!"
Reality: More revenue does not automatically change the bottom line. It is much more about the revenue you keep than the revenue you earn. Therefore, you should first concentrate on the margin earned on revenue.

Myth 2: "Financial success is based on how much product the company sells."
Reality: As stated above, financial success is not a function of top line earnings, rather, it is a function of how much money the company keeps (the margin). All revenue before margin is just a "pass through."

Myth 3: "Inflation makes borrowing wise because it allows the company to buy what it needs now and pay it off later when money is worth less."
Reality: Debt is bondage and should be avoided whenever possible. Whenever you borrow money, you create a real liability to the lending entity. To more fully understand this, you need only look at how the federal government operates.

Myth 4: "Once in debt, it is almost impossible to get out."
Reality: Any debt that can be incurred can be erased. The first step is to alter your borrowing habits, and then make sure that your margins will support the pay down of already incurred debt.

Myth 5: "If the economy was better we would be making more money."
Reality: Blaming the economy for company problems is the first step toward ultimate disaster. Long-term success means operating profitably in both good and bad economies.

These are just some of the more common money myths encountered in operating a successful business. Understanding the difference between the myth and reality is crucial for operational success.

Business Structures

Types of Business Structures

Businesses can be structured in more than one way; each has its advantages and disadvantages. Deciding which one is right for you should involve discussions with your attorney and your accountant. Some structures have debt liability advantages, while others do not. It is important to select the right structure for your situation. Here are the structures commonly used:

Sole Proprietorship: This is simple and inexpensive to create and operate. The owner is personally liable for business debts and reports profit or loss on his or her personal tax return, so the company does not pay a separate income tax. This structure provides neither liability protection from creditors nor tax advantages.

Partnership: Partnerships can be general or limited. They are simple and inexpensive to create and operate. The owners (partners) are personally liable for business debts and report their share of profits or losses on their personal tax returns. From a debt liability and tax standpoint this works just like a sole proprietorship.

Closed Corporation (C Corp): This is the standard business structure for many corporations. The business has shareholders and the owners (shareholders) have limited personal liability for business debts. This structure is more expensive to create than other business structures, and the paperwork can seem burdensome to some owners. The business operates as a separate taxable entity, so taxable income does not flow to the stockholders' personal tax returns. Stockholders are taxed on distributions of corporate income only. Since the corporation pays income tax on the profits and the stockholders pay income tax on any distributions of the profits, the corporate profits are subject to double taxation.

Subchapter S Corporation (S Corp): This corporation operates like a partnership, but with limited liability, and has become much more common in recent years. An S Corp usually has a small number of owners who are issued stock certificates. Owners report their share of profits or losses on their personal tax returns and are taxed on their share of profits as determined by their share of ownership. This structure does provide debt liability to owners.

Limited Liability Company (LLC): Like a partnership or sole proprietorship, but with limited debt liability, an LLC is easy to form with limited reporting needed. There are no stock certificates; owners report their share of profits or losses on their personal tax returns. Owners enter into an operating agreement that defines each owner's share of ownership and how the company will operate. That share of ownership determines how much of the company profit carries through to each owner's personal tax return.

Reading and Understanding Financial Statements

The two basic financial statements of any company are the income statement, also known as the profit and loss statement, and the balance sheet. All actions, decisions, and choices that are made on a daily basis will eventually be reflected on either the income statement or balance sheet. There are many other business reports, all generated by basic accounting software, but a full understanding of both the income statement and the balance sheet is essential to understanding the financial health of any company. (I will not cover the other reports available as this would take too long and is really not necessary for most small business owners.) The first step in understanding financial statements is to understand the basic terminology.

Standard Business Terminology

Debit: an increase in an expense or asset or a decrease in revenue, net worth, or liability.

Credit: a decrease in assets or expenses or an increase in revenue, equity or liabilities; also an arrangement for deferred payment for goods and services. You can both extend credit to customers and receive credit from vendors and lenders.

Asset: land, equipment, building, cash, investments, etc.

Liability: debt owed to someone or some entity.

Revenue: gross sales or proceeds (also called turnover).

Expenses: also known as overhead, these are costs not directly associated with the generation of revenue such as utilities, insurance, taxes, administrative salaries, maintenance costs, and so on.

Cost of Goods Sold (COGS): costs directly associated with the generation of revenue, such as parts, materials, labor, fringe benefits, and other direct costs.

Gross Margin: Revenue less COGS, the critical indicator of profitability.

Margin Percentage: Gross Margin divided by Revenue.

Profit and Loss Statement (P&L): the most basic statement of profitability, broken down into three sections, income, cost of goods sold, and expenses.

Balance Sheet: statement of company assets, liabilities, and equity. Assets always equal total liabilities plus total equity.

Net profit: gross margin minus all expenses.

Measures of Business Operations

Return on sales (net profit/revenue): Basic measure of profitability.

Return on equity (net profit /equity): Measures owners' return on their investment.

Labor to sales percentage (labor costs/total revenue): Measures the percentage of revenue that is consumed in direct labor costs.

Return on assets (net profit/net total assets): Measures how effective the company is in utilizing its assets.

Liquidity Measures: Current ratio, quick ratio, acid test

Current ratio (current assets/current liabilities): Measures a company's ability to meet its demand for operating funds. Any ratio greater than one means the company has sufficient current assets to meet its short-term obligations.

Quick ratio ((current assets − inventory)/current liabilities): A more stringent measure of a company's ability to meet short-term funding needs. Inventory is considered not immediately convertible into cash.

Acid test (cash/current liabilities): The most stringent measure of short-term operating funds. A ratio greater than one means the company has sufficient cash on hand to meet short-term operating needs (i.e., pay its bills).

Debt Ratios: Debt to assets, debt to equity

Debt to assets (debt/assets): Measures the company's ability to fund its long-term debt from assets. Assets would not normally be used to fund debt; profitability does that. However, lenders look at this ratio to see how debt could ultimately be funded.

Debt to equity (debt/equity): Measures the company's debt against accumulated equity and indicates the long-term viability of the company. A debt ratio greater than one indicates a heavily indebted company.

Operations: ADRO, ADPO, Asset turnover, break-even point

ADRO or Average Days Receivables Outstanding (receivables/(revenue/365)): Measures how long your customers are taking, on average, to make payments. This must be looked at with regard to your payment terms. If your terms are net thirty days to your customers, then an ADRO less than thirty means that, on average, your customers are paying you within your terms.

ADPO or Average Days Payables Outstanding (accounts payable/(COGS/365)): Measures how long it is taking you to pay your vendors. This is a snapshot and must be looked at over time. It is also important to try to match ADPO to ADRO so that you are not in need of short-term borrowing.

Asset turnover (revenue/assets): A general indicator of how much revenue your assets are generating. The higher the ratio, the more revenue your assets are generating.

Break-even point: the revenue point at which gross margin exactly covers overhead (see computation below.)

The Income Statement

The income statement, also known as the profit and loss statement, is the one report on which we all tend to focus our attention since it provides the proverbial "bottom line"—the company's profit or loss. Usually done on a monthly, quarterly, and yearly basis, the income statement is divided into three sections.

The first section is the revenue section. To compute total revenues, add all of the revenue items and subtract any deductions from revenue. These deductions could be in the form of rebates or discounts on goods or services sold.

The next section is cost of goods sold, the total costs associated with the generation of revenue. These costs normally include materials and labor costs. They can also include other types of costs directly associated with the generation of revenue. For example, some income statements include fringe benefits in cost of goods sold since fringe benefits are generally paid based on labor costs.

The percentage of gross margin to revenues is a very useful number. It can help you compare yourself with other companies in your industry; in doing so it tells you whether your costs, for labor and other items, are in or out of line with industry averages. Also, continually tracking gross margin percentage allows a comparison between your current production efficiency with previous your efficiency from previous periods. This allows you to keep comparing "apples to apples" from one period to another.

The third section deals with overhead or expenses, including items such as insurance, utilities, salaries, travel expenses, depreciation, and so forth. Subtract all of these expense items from gross margin to get net profit before taxes. There is no universally accepted percentage that your pretax net profit must be, though higher is obviously better.

From net profit before taxes, subtract a provision for taxes and the result, at long last, is your net income or loss. You must have profit sufficient to allow for reinvestment of the profits back into the company to meet capital expenditure needs for future growth and also to retire existing debt. Only after all other needs for capital are met can you then address distribution of any profits to ownership.

Keep in mind that for many small businesses, the income statement is less important than the cash-flow statement, since it's possible for a business to run out of cash even though it is actually profitable. For example, if your customers are taking too long to pay (ADRO is over forty-five days) while your vendors are demanding fifteen- or twenty-day payment terms, you can run short of cash. This may necessitate short-term borrowing to satisfy operational needs for cash; even while the income statement shows a profit. The company may also need cash investments in fixed assets. You don't want to have to borrow money every time you need a computer.

If a portion of the previous year's profitability has not been set aside for capital investment, then the company will frequently be short of cash. This may again necessitate borrowing. As stated before, this borrowing would occur notwithstanding profitability as shown on the income statement. The primary difference, then, between cash flow and profitability on the income statement is timing.

Just as important as timing of cash flow is knowing your break-even point. It helps you understand your current situation and allows you to make adjustments to your operations. Here is how to calculate your break-even point:

Determine your monthly fixed costs (overhead).
Determine your gross margin percentage.
Divide your fixed costs by your margin percentage.

Example: Bob wants to know what monthly revenue will be sufficient to cover his overhead of $80,000 per month. He has already determined that his gross margin percentage is 40 percent. So he divides $80,000 by 40 percent and now knows that he must have $200,000 per month to cover his fixed costs (to break even).

Note: I hope you can see that there are two variables in determining the break-even point. A positive effect on either variable will lower the break-even point: effective expense control or increased production efficiency. After the break-even point is achieved, all gross margin realized is pretax profit!

Here is an example of a basic income statement. Even though it is very simple, it is representative of what you will find on most companies' financials. These statements can get very long and seem complicated, but remember they still break down into the three sections: income, cost of goods sold, and expenses.

Income Statement
ABC Company

Revenue	$1,234,567
Less: Returns	7,654
Net Sales	1,226,913
Cost of Goods Sold:	
Materials	163,598
Variable Labor	495,613
Total Cost of Goods Sold	659,211
Gross Profit	567,702
Expenses:	
Advertising	7,541
Payroll	98,365
Payroll Taxes and Benefits	13,240

Sales Commissions	25,324
Professional Fees	10,201
Operating Supplies	23,324
Travel	6,510
Communications	8,654
Maintenance and Repairs	18,686
Office Supplies	8,988
Miscellaneous	15,896
Permits and Licenses	4,503
Interest	8,610
Depreciation	33,824
Property Taxes	8,724
Rent	9,800
Insurance	12,500
Utilities	25,666
Bad Debts	100
Bank Service Charges	760
Total Expenses	341,216
Net Operating Income	226,486
Other Income:	
Gain (Loss) on Sale of Assets	1,200
Interest Income	325
Total Other Income	1,525
Net Income (Loss)	228,011
Taxes	79,804
Net Income after Taxes	$148,207

As you can see, this example income statement shows a profitable company. It has a net after-tax profit of $148,207, which is 12 percent of revenue. That is pretty good—most companies have net after-tax profits of less than 10 percent. This provides funds to reinvest in the company. In small businesses most owners simply reinvest their profits back into their company year after year.

The owner's compensation is included in payroll. The owner would need to look carefully at upcoming capital investment needs before taking any additional compensation in the form of a distribution of profits.

The Balance Sheet

The next statement is the balance sheet. Here is an example of a basic balance sheet. It is also very simple but still representative of what you will find on most company's financials. The balance sheets of large corporations are always long and complicated. (I think they do this purposely to confuse the general public.) Nevertheless, they still break down into these three sections: assets, liabilities, and equity.

Balance Sheet
ABC Company
As of 6/30/2014

Assets
Current Assets
Cash (Your bank account)	$351,253
Accounts Receivable	164,359
Less: Allowance for bad debts	500
Merchandise Inventory	126,395
Prepaid Expenses	15,493
Note Receivable	958
Total Current Assets	$657,958

Fixed Assets
Vehicles	$48,294
Less: Accumulated Depreciation	(13,658)

Net Vehicles	34,636
Furniture & Fixtures	84,352
Less: Accumulated Depreciation	(29,740)
Net Furniture & Fixtures	54,612
Equipment	198,264
Less: Accumulated Depreciation	(38,204)
Net Equipment	160,060
Total Fixed Assets	$249,308
Total Assets	**$907,266**

Liabilities
Current Liabilities

Accounts Payable	$14,310
Sales Tax Payable	13,209
Payroll Tax Payable	20,023
Income Tax Payable	8,974
Accrued Wages Payable	6,155
Total Current Liabilities	$62,671

Long-Term Liabilities

Note Payable	201,154
Total Long-Term Liabilities	$201,154
Total Liabilities	**$263,825**

Equity

Common Stock	$84,212
Retained Earnings – Prior Years	503,224
Net Income – Current Year	56,005
Total Equity	**$643,441**
Total Liabilities & Equity	**$907,266**

The balance sheet shows the state of the company's assets and liabilities at a particular point in time. It is a snapshot that changes every time you take it. As a statement of the company's resources, it is important in determining basic business health. Like the income statement, it is also composed of three sections.

Assets

Section one shows the company's assets: current assets such as cash, accounts receivable, or short-term loans receivable and fixed assets such as buildings, equipment, land, furniture, computers, and so on. These are all additions to a company's asset base.

The balance sheet also contains deductions from a company's asset base in the form of depreciation. (Depreciation is an allocated expense for previous capital expenditures.) By adding together all of the company's assets as shown on its balance sheet and subtracting all the depreciation of those assets, you are arrive at a book value of total net assets. In this example the total assets are $907,266.

Liabilities

The second section shows liabilities, which are composed of current liabilities and long-term liabilities. Items such as accounts payable, short-term debt, and accrued expense items are examples of current liabilities. In addition to current liabilities, the balance sheet will more than likely include a section on long-term liabilities: generally long-term debt (borrowing) incurred in the operation of the company. Adding current liabilities to long-term liabilities gives you the company's total liabilities. In this example the total liabilities are $263,825.

Equity

The third section is the equity section, which shows the amount of initial investment, stock ownership amounts, and retained earnings. It may also show deductions from retained earnings in the form of distributions. In this example the total equity is $643,441.

From an accounting perspective, the equity section of the balance sheet simply reconciles total assets and total liabilities. This is to say that total assets must always be equal to the sum of total liabilities and owners' equity. This is the balancing that takes place.

Balance sheets are useful measurements of the health of manufacturing, wholesaling, and other product-oriented businesses in which assets can be measured in terms of equipment and inventory. (They are somewhat less useful for evaluating service-only businesses since these businesses have not much in terms of equipment and inventory.) You can see that this company is not only profitable in the current year (net income) but also has long-term profitability (retained earnings – prior years). The company should be able to borrow money, as it has equity of $643,441 and assets of $907,266 against liabilities of only $263,825.

Bankers tend to rely heavily on balance sheets, using ratios of various assets and liabilities to determine the health of a company. As the economy becomes more service oriented, though, bankers are gradually changing their attitudes, so it pays to shop around for a banker who will understand your business and is willing to work with you. In my experience, bankers only look at the income statement after they have looked at and fully analyzed the balance sheet.

Analysis of Financial Statements

The balance sheet and the income statement are essential, but they are only the starting points for successful financial management. It is important to apply ratio analysis to financial statements to analyze the success, failure, and progress of your company. This enables you to spot trends in a company and to compare its performance with the performance of similar businesses in the same industry.

In addition to comparing your company's ratios with similar companies in the same industry, you must also compare your current ratios with the ratios from prior years. By continually comparing your current period's ratios to ratios from prior periods, you can get a very strong picture of your company's trends, whether good or bad. Ratio analysis may provide the early warning indications that allow you to address your business problems before they become unresolvable.

Balance Sheet Analysis

Important balance sheet ratios measure liquidity, which is a business's ability to pay its bills on time, as well as measuring leverage. Liquidity ratios are indicators of how easily a company can turn assets into cash. They include measures such as the current ratio, the quick ratio, and the acid test. Leverage is the extent to which a business is dependent on debt financing and is measured by working capital and leverage ratios. Too much debt can overburden a company, making it impossible for the company to both service its debt and continue to invest in the company's future.

Liquidity Measures

The current ratio is one of the best-known measures of liquidity. The calculation is shown below:

$$\text{Current Ratio} = \frac{\text{Total Current Assets}}{\text{Total Current Liabilities}}$$

Current ratio addresses the question, "Does your company have sufficient current assets to meet its current obligations without short-term borrowing?" A generally acceptable current ratio is two (meaning two to one). That is two dollars of current assets for every dollar of current liabilities. Whether or not a specific ratio is sufficient depends on the characteristics of your current assets and liabilities. The more cash you have on hand, as opposed to a larger amount of accounts receivable, the stronger your position to meet your current liability obligations. The minimum acceptable current ratio for a healthy business is one to one, generally expressed as simply the number one.

The quick ratio is also a good measure of liquidity. The calculation is shown below:

$$\text{Quick Ratio} = \frac{\text{Current Assets} - \text{Inventories}}{\text{Total Current Liabilities}}$$

The quick ratio is a more stringent measure of liquidity than the current ratio. Inventories are excluded from it because they are considered somewhat difficult to turn into immediate cash. A quick ratio of one (meaning one to one) says you do not need to liquidate your inventory in order to pay your current obligations. A caveat to this would be if a significant majority of current assets are accounts receivable, as opposed to cash on hand. The quick ratio addresses the question, "If all revenues disappear, can we pay our current obligations with the readily convertible funds (current assets) on hand?"

The most stringent measure of liquidity is the acid test. The calculation is shown below:

$$\text{Acid Test} = \frac{\text{Cash}}{\text{Current Liabilities}}$$

An acid test of one (meaning one to one) is very satisfactory, though not common. It is more likely that your acid test number will be less than one. Be careful that it does not get so low that you do not have sufficient cash to sustain an ongoing operation. If this happens, you must then go to the bank to exercise a line of credit (a short-term loan).

In general, the higher these three liquidity ratios are the better, especially if you are relying on creditor money to finance assets.

If you decide that your liquidity measures are too low, you may be able to raise them by:

- Paying some short-term debts (current liabilities).
- Increasing your cash provided by loans by converting short-term borrowing to long-term borrowing.
- Increasing your current assets from new equity contributions (owners' infusion of capital).
- Putting profits back into the business (lowering or eliminating stock dividends or owners' draws).

Your goal should not be to change liquidity measures as an exercise in academic improvement but to improve liquidity for operational purposes. The higher your liquidity the less you worry about "keeping the doors open." You can concentrate on improving other areas, such as production efficiency or customer service.

Leverage

Working capital is more a measure of cash flow than a ratio. The result of this calculation must be a positive number. It is calculated as shown below:

Working Capital = Total Current Assets − Total Current Liabilities

The larger the amount of working capital a company has, the greater its ability to fund ongoing operations without incurring additional short-term debt. You should ensure that you have sufficient working capital to provide for at least several months of continuing operation, though this is highly dependent upon the industry in which you operate; working capital may be significantly higher in production industries than in service industries.

Leverage ratios indicate the extent to which the business is reliant on debt financing and can be viewed as creditor money versus owners' equity. They are calculated as shown below:

$$\text{Equity Leverage Ratio} = \frac{\text{Long-Term Debt}}{\text{Equity}}$$

$$\text{Asset Leverage Ratio} = \frac{\text{Long-Term Debt}}{\text{Assets}}$$

Generally, as these ratios increase, creditors or bankers perceive exposure in your business as more risky, making it correspondingly harder to obtain credit or loans. Obviously, a leverage ratio less than one is highly desirable.

Income Statement Analysis

Income statement analysis allows you to analyze and understand profitability. There are several different calculations. I have found the ones those listed below to be the most useful in understanding the efficiency of production and overall administrative efficiency.

Gross Margin Percentage: The percentage of sales dollars left after subtracting the cost of goods sold from net sales. It measures the percentage of sales dollars remaining (after obtaining or manufacturing the goods sold), which are available to pay the overhead expenses of the company and provide for profitability.

This percentage is best used to compare your current operations to operations in previous periods or to compare the efficiency of your operation to other businesses in your industry. It is calculated as shown below:

$$\text{Gross Margin Percentage} = \frac{(\text{Total Revenue} - \text{COGS})}{\text{Total Revenue}}$$

As you can see, total revenue minus the total cost of goods sold gives you the gross margin. The percentage is computed by dividing gross margin by total revenue. For example, a company has total revenues of $1,000,000 and total cost of goods sold of $600,000. Subtracting the $600,000 from the $1,000,000 will give you a gross margin of $400,000. Dividing the gross margin of $400,000 by $1,000,000 of total revenue results in a gross margin of 40 percent.

It is difficult for a company to be very profitable if its gross margin percentage is not at least 40 percent, though this varies from one industry to the next, and some high-volume industries can operate on lower gross margin percentages. For example, insurance and travel agencies regularly operate with margins of only around 10 percent. With high enough volumes and low overhead, they can still turn a nice profit. However, you should always strive to increase your gross margin to the highest extent possible.

Net Profit Percentage: This ratio is the percentage of total revenue remaining after subtracting the cost of goods sold and all expenses, except income taxes. It is commonly known as your "return on sales." This is a pretax calculation that allows you to compare the performance of your company with that of other companies in the same industry. It is calculated as shown below:

$$\text{NP Percentage} = \frac{\text{Total Revenue} - (\text{COGS} + \text{Expenses})}{\text{Total Revenue}}$$

Net profit percentage varies widely from one industry to another. However, you should strive for a percentage in excess of 10 percent before taxes. This is a generalization and may not always be possible, but it is a good benchmark to shoot for.

In analyzing the income statement, I always convert all items below the revenue line to a percentage of total revenue. This allows you to compare numbers over time and against previous periods and makes it very easy to identify areas in which expenses are increasing (the percentages will be increasing).

Working capital, leverage ratio, gross margin, and gross margin percentage are the four numbers that tell you a lot about the current health of your company. Focus on them first.

Additional Ratios

Other important ratios can also be derived from balance sheet and income statement information.

Inventory turnover indicates the efficiency of inventory management. It is important because the more times inventory can be turned in any given operating cycle, the less the costs of carrying that inventory, and the greater the profit on that inventory. It is calculated as follows:

$$\text{Inventory Turnover} = \frac{\text{Total Revenue}}{\text{Average Inventory at Cost}}$$

So, look at your balance sheet at the end of each month and average the month-end inventory value over the previous year. Then divide that number into the total revenue for the year. This will give your number of inventory turns per year. The more turns you get, the more you will make on that inventory investment.

Average Days Receivables Outstanding (ADRO) measures your effectiveness in collecting monies owed to the company. If receivables are not collected reasonably in accordance with your terms, you should look closely at your terms and collection policies. ADRO is calculated as follows:

$$ADRO = \frac{\text{Total Accounts Receivable Outstanding}}{(\text{Total Annual Revenue}/365)}$$

The balance sheet shows the current accounts receivable number. The income statement shows the total revenue, which you then annualize. These two numbers are then used in the computation, as shown above. This is one of your more critical numbers, as it shows how capable you are at maintaining needed cash flow without short-term borrowing.

As previously stated, if your ADRO is forty-five, this means your customers are paying you within forty-five days of the invoice date, on average. However, you still have wages and salaries to pay, and it is not likely your employees will let you pay them once every forty-five days. It is also unlikely your vendors will be happy about you always taking forty-five days to pay them. Therefore, it is very important to keep your ADRO number as close to your payment terms as possible.

I cannot overstate the importance of closely monitoring this number. It can mean the difference between always drawing on a line of credit and never doing so. Remember, credit may be readily available, but it is not free.

Return on assets measures how efficiently profits are being generated from company assets. A low percentage in comparison with the industry average can indicate an inefficient use of company assets. It is calculated as follows:

$$\text{Return on Assets} = \frac{\text{Net Profit before Tax}}{\text{Total Assets}}$$

As with most other measures, it is important to track this number over time. It is unlikely to vary much from month to month or even quarter to quarter. But it can vary significantly from year to year, depending on production efficiency and asset purchases or disposals. Take a long-term view of this measure.

Return on investment (ROI) is frequently considered the most important measure of all. It is the percentage of return on funds invested in the business by its owners. The ROI is calculated as follows:

$$ROI = \frac{\text{Net Profit before Taxes}}{\text{Owners' Equity}}$$

In short, this ratio tells you whether or not all the effort put into the business has been worthwhile in strictly financial terms. If your ROI is less than the rate of return on a risk-free investment, such as a bank savings account, it may be attractive (financially) to sell the company, put the money in such a financial instrument, and go your merry way.

It is my experience that the owners of small business rarely look at their investment in strictly financial terms. There is real, yet uncalculated, value to many people to own their own business. I find ROI to be a good measure for comparison purposes but rarely used by small business owners in deciding whether or not to sell their business.

These management measures allow you to identify trends in your company. They should be used to compare your progress over time and your performance with the performance of other companies in your industry. This takes both diligence and vigilance. Make a spreadsheet and track these measures monthly. However, look at them over a longer time period than just one month. You must decide which of these measures is most important to you, and know what you can do to positively impact those measures.

Understanding Cash Flow

All business owners understand cash flow from an emotional perspective. However, to many managers, cash flow is not much more than the balance in the company's operating (bank) account. So let's take a closer look at cash flow since it is critical to success in any business. Cash flow is what keeps the doors open regardless of whether or not there is short-term profitability. (If there is not long-term profitability, then the company has an even bigger problem.) As was previously stated, it is possible to be profitable and not be able to pay your bills. If this occurs, there is a significant problem with cash flow in your business.

I once heard that it might be useful to understand cash flow by looking at a business as a living organism. In fact it is very important to understand that the business does function and operate separately from ownership. This is to say that ownership is not the business; the business is a separate entity from ownership.

If we do in fact look at business as a living organism, then cash is the blood that runs through the circulatory system of the organism. So then you might think of the brain as the combination of the goods and services provided (operations), along with the management team. The heart of the organism would be sales and marketing since it is pumping revenue into the system. The nourishment of the organism (digestive system) would be provided by finance.

This rather crude analogy makes it very easy to understand that the brain, the heart, and the nourishment system cannot operate without blood (cash) flowing through the circulatory system. If you don't have enough cash flow, the business dies a relatively short, yet painful, death. Hence the expression, "The company is bleeding cash."

The essential point about cash flow is that it is different from profit and, in the short run, more important. At the time of this writing, the federal government is shut down due to a fight between Congress and the President over the budget. Congress is insisting on reductions in spending before passing a continuing resolution to keep the government running. Another battle looming in the federal government right now is the battle over raising the debt ceiling.

If these two issues were looked at in business terms, the budget battle is a battle for profitability (in the case of the federal government it is the lack thereof), and the battle over raising the debt ceiling is a battle over short-term cash flow. This is an analogy that all business owners should understand fully. That is to say, it's possible to run out of cash even if you have significant sales because you aren't being paid in a timely way. So profitability and cash flow can never be divorced from each other, but cash flow can keep the doors open while you are working on profitability.

Let's say your company manufactures and sells large-ticket items, worth in excess of $50,000. Once you receive an order, the delivery process begins. To manufacture the product, you must cut purchase orders to vendors and begin the production and assembly process before delivery to the customer. This process could take anywhere from three to six months or even longer.

In the meantime you have to pay your labor costs, and you also must pay the vendors that provided the raw materials or assembly parts for use in the production process. This becomes a significant cash-flow issue in many companies especially if it takes six months between the time an order is received from the customer and the time a product is delivered. On top of this, you might need to add the amount of time that it will take for the customer to remit payment to you. This then might become a cash-flow dilemma.

The challenge is not that the item sold by the salesperson is not a profitable item. However, it does create a challenge to cash flow during the production, delivery, and receipt of payment process.

Cash flow should also be used as a planning tool. By monitoring cash flow on a regular basis as cash comes in and goes out, you'll see a pattern that enables you to plan for the future. This is very important, especially if you want to expand, as this might change your cash flow. You can quickly calculate the effect of any actions on cash flow and determine whether you'll need to get a bank loan or whether you can support the expansion from ongoing operations.

Calculating Cash Flow

Quite simply, cash flow is a record of cash available at different points in times, usually monitored on a monthly basis. A cash-flow statement seems complicated at first glance, but it's really very simple.

Begin with the cash on hand at the beginning of the month; add receipts during the month from monies coming into the company; and subtract the cash disbursements—the cash going out each month to cover ongoing operations. The result is the amount of cash available at the end of the month. The cash flow is the difference between what you started with and what you ended with.

These cash disbursements can be either fixed or variable. For example, rent is a fixed expense, while hourly labor is a variable expense. Fixed expenses generally cannot be changed; variable expenses can be changed to meet your cash-flow requirements.

Cash-flow calculation can get very complicated depending on the multitude of inputs that go into it. However, no matter how many factors go into the calculation, the basic formula remains: Cash on hand, plus cash received, minus cash disbursed.

The Cash-Flow Statement

I believe that all accounting software contains a cash-flow statement used to identify when cash is expected to be received and when it must be spent. It should also show how much cash will be needed and when it will be needed. This enables management to plan for shortfalls in available cash so short-term loans (lines of credit) can be arranged. It allows you to schedule purchases and payments in a way that enables the business to borrow only when necessary.

Most businesses operate on an accrual basis: a product or service is provided, and the customer is invoiced for the same. Therefore, cash is not immediately received for a sale. You must then be able to estimate when accounts receivable will be turned into cash and when expenses must be paid. The goal is to try to avoid running short of the cash you need to operate. This analysis helps identify areas for needed improvement in managing your company finances, such as improving accounts receivable collections.

One of the most basic methods of managing cash flow is to match receivables (ADRO) to payables (ADPO). This is the fundamental reason these two numbers are calculated. By closely watching ADRO and ADPO you can see whether there is a problem with customers taking too long to pay. This is the most common problem I have encountered in managing cash flow in any business. If your customers are taking too long to remit payment to you, you may need to look carefully at your collections systems. It is very critical to try to time cash receivables to match cash disbursements so that the revenue received from your operations finances your ongoing operations.

If you have surplus cash, that surplus may then be used to reduce debt, thereby reducing interest expense. Should you need a short-term loan, bankers will look carefully at your cash flow and pay particular attention to how many days it takes you to collect from your customers. After all, bankers will only lend money when they have a strong assurance of being repaid and an understanding of your ability to repay. As a thirty-year veteran of the banking business explained to me, bankers really want to lend money—but only to companies that don't really need to borrow it.

It is essential that you realize that cash flow and profitability are equally vital to business success. Matching receivables and payables is a never-ending process. Failure to monitor both may necessitate short-term borrowing that carries with it additional cost. Be diligent in cash-flow management, and you will sleep easier at night.

How to Effectively Manage Working Capital

Managing working capital in a small business is very different than that of large corporations, even though the fundamentals are the same. So what is working capital?

Working Capital generally consists of:

(1) Cash and equivalents (liquid)
(2) Accounts receivable (somewhat liquid)
(3) Inventories (not very liquid)
(4) Accounts payable (to vendors)
(5) Notes payable (on loans)
(6) Accrued expenses (insurance, taxes, etc.)

In dollar terms, net working capital is the difference between current assets and current liabilities. If you divide current assets by current liabilities, the result is your working capital ratio (also known as the current ratio). The higher the ratio, the more working capital a company has. A ratio less than 1.0 means a company may not have sufficient capital to fund current operations—literally may not have sufficient funds to pay its creditors. Ideally, you would like to have a working capital ratio of 1.5 or more to fund ongoing operations. On the other hand, too much working capital could be an indicator that the company is not investing sufficiently for the long term. Failure to effectively manage working capital is a primary cause of business failures in both small and large companies.

Small business owners primarily rely on credit from vendors, bank financing (if possible), and leasing and personal investment to finance their businesses. Since strict limitations are placed on small businesses from external financing sources, they face a more severely limited set of alternatives than large companies do. At the same time, both small and big businesses face similar challenges. The large corporation simply has more alternatives available to it.

For example, let's say a company needs to purchase a piece of capital equipment, like a boiler or a furnace. The decision process for whether or not to purchase the equipment is probably much the same whether the company is large or small. Large companies may just have more people involved in the process. However, once the decision to purchase is made, the working capital alternatives for the purchase may vary radically between a small company and a large company.

The small company generally has two choices. The owners either have the money in savings to make the purchase, or they go to the bank and try to borrow the funds.

The large company can also self-finance or go to a bank, but it may also look to issue corporate bonds, issue stock (either common or preferred), look for a third party capital infusion, or set up a lease program, among other options. Generally, these other options are not available to a small company. These limitations highlight the need for small business owners to manage working capital effectively. With limited options comes a limited allowance for errors.

An effective manager must be continually alert to changes in working capital. The manager must first find out what has caused those changes. So an analysis of the account changes must be performed. The manager is also going to want to know the overall trend in working capital. Is it up or is it down? Which accounts are responsible for the trend? If the trend is negative, what can be done to correct it?

If your company has a great many physical assets (buildings and equipment), it is critical to estimate when you will need to replace one or more of those assets. At the time of replacement, how will you finance that capital expenditure? Is your current system for growing your working capital sufficient to meet future challenges, or do changes need to be made? Does your banker understand how your business operates and, by extension, how the bank can help to meet your future capital needs?

It is only by devoting time and effort to tracking changes in working capital and then projecting those changes (trends) forward that you can ensure that sufficient working capital will be available for future needs.

Here are some basic questions to help with the process of managing working capital:

- Do you have, or have access to, sufficient working capital to meet company needs for the next three years?
- What changes are taking place in the working capital accounts?
- What can be done to positively affect working capital by more carefully managing change?
- Are you going to borrow or self-finance to meet future needs?
- If you plan to self-finance, how much must you set aside in a savings account to meet future needs?
- If you must borrow, have you established a good relationship with a lender who understands your business?

- How will an improvement in margin positively affect working capital, and how long will that improvement take to show a significant increase in working capital?

This is a summary of the process of managing working capital. Although much has been written about proper working capital management, the fundamentals are simple: you must continually project forward your working capital needs and plan to meet those needs.

Effective Collection Methods

Accounts receivables are very important assets of any company. However, they can also be very strenuous and frustrating when it comes to collecting those accounts. A systematic approach is key to effective collection. You will find that most customers with whom you do business are fully intent on paying your invoices on time and try to adhere to your payment terms. I have found that the majority of problems in the accounts receivable collection process arise because of technical issues such as missed purchase order numbers, incorrect purchase order numbers, incorrect addresses, missing approvals, and so on. These are all just a failure to properly complete paperwork.

It is important that the collection process always be professional. This is not a place for emotion or for questioning anyone's integrity. Your payment terms policy must be both reasonable and openly communicated to your customers. You can't expect your customers to adhere to your payment terms if they are not of aware of those terms. Standard payment terms are net thirty days, but you could have other payment terms that better fit your needs.

Communication is important, and it must be consistent and businesslike. After all, you want customers who owe you money to pay you and at the same time to continue to do business with you. It is of little value to collect money from a customer if in doing so you irritate him to such an extent that he will no longer do business with you. You will find that a professional collection system will not only work properly but will also help to ensure that your current customers will remain your future customers. So be firm, but be pleasant.

Unfortunately, some companies will not readily adhere to your payment terms without being prodded to do so. However, it is the nature of how you go about this prodding that not only helps you collect the monies owed you but also makes you a priority in your customers' minds. Think of the vendors with which you do business and how important it is for you to maintain a professional relationship with them. You must make sure that your vendor's invoices are paid on time if you want them to keep providing goods and services to you. It is the same with monies owed to you since you are the vendor to your customers.

It is important to establish and document a collections policy. That policy must be followed throughout the collections process, as this will ensure that your customers become familiar with how you do business and what they can expect from you. In establishing your policy, answer some basic questions:

- Are you going to send out statements once a month or twice a month?
- Are you going to follow up on the statements each time they are sent, or only occasionally?
- What will your follow-up system be?

These are questions that must be answered in order to establish an effective collections policy.

Most companies have come to expect a payment terms policy of net thirty days or greater. The problem with this is that your vendors usually expect you to pay them in thirty days or less. Therein lies an obvious dilemma. You must manage the difference between what your customers expect and what your vendors expect. Without an effective and well-established collections policy, it can be very challenging to manage these expectations.

The first step of an effective collection system is making sure that your invoices are sent out in a timely manner. The sooner an invoice is sent, the sooner you will receive payment for the services. Also, this portrays your operating system as professional to your customers.

Additionally, I have found that sending statements out on the first of every month, after the previous month's close, is very effective. Someone must go over the statements individually and note any past due balances on the statement itself. If you don't bring these past due balances to your customers' attention, they are likely to overlook the statement as being insignificant. A simple way to note these past due balances is to use a highlighter for any amounts that are past due. I also make use of a large "Past Due" stamp on all statements with a past due balance.

Once the invoices have gone out promptly and the statements have been sent (duly marked), you can focus on the customers that are past due. If you have a policy of net thirty days, it is not productive to spend time on payments that are only ten or fifteen days past due. It is not realistic to expect your customer's accounts payable system to adhere to your payment terms to the exact day.

Today most everyone has an e-mail address. Statements can be sent via e-mail, as can any follow-up communication. Any customer who is sixty days or more past due should receive not only a statement but also an e-mail and a phone call. The phone call and e-mail must be professional and courteous, a simple enquiry as to when the referenced invoices will be paid.

Evernote™ is a good system for making notes of both e-mails and phone conversations. It can be organized by customer name and by chronological event to help you track who was spoken to, what was said, when it was said, and what was the agreed upon next step. This is where diligence is important. In a conversation with a customer, if that customer states that an invoice or series invoices will be paid within the next "xx" days, it is imperative to check whether or not that payment was received as promised. If the payment was not received within that period of time, it is just as important to follow up again with that customer and remind him or her of the previous commitment.

All correspondence sent must show your company name and contact information. The contact person's name must also be provided as well as a return telephone number and e-mail address. This lets your customer know that you are serious and makes it easier to respond to you. Be sure to reiterate the payment terms as well as your expectations. If you don't tell the customer what you expect, how can you possibly expect the customer to abide by your terms? Again, be courteous, but be firm.

Now that your invoices and your statements have been sent, you must focus on systematic communications. Your customers will come to expect communication from you on a regular basis only if you do in fact communicate with them on that basis. If you do not adhere to a schedule of communications, your invoices tend to go to the bottom of the pile.

I have found the most effective method of collection is a telephone call: you can speak directly with someone in your customer's accounts payable department and correct any technical issues that may have kept your invoices from being paid. Regular telephone communication also establishes a relationship with your customer and is helpful in any resolving any issues. While you may occasionally use collection letters, they are generally unnecessary if you have made phone calls and sent e-mails.

This multistep approach of sending out invoices followed by statements followed by e-mails and phone calls has proven to be the most effective method in collecting monies owed. This is not to say that everyone will adhere to your payment terms or will be motivated to pay all your invoices on time. However, it is only after these normal methods of communication are exhausted that other remedies should be sought.

While it sounds great in theory, the reality is that not all customers will be treated equally. You are likely to treat the customer that only deals with you occasionally and is frequently past due much differently from your best customer who may also be frequently past due. This is where reasonableness and common sense must come into the collections process. While both customers must pay you, it is unlikely you will be as aggressive in collections with your best customer as you will be with the occasional customer. You do want to pay special attention to any customers owing large amounts of money, but you also want to ensure they will continue to be your customers. Be firm, but be reasonable.

Reasonableness means allowing for the human factor in any transaction as you systemize your collections process. Sometimes the key to getting paid is nothing more than making sure the invoice gets to the right people. If your collections process is done correctly, your cash flow will improve, and your relationships with customers will be solidified. These are both key to long-term success.

Below are two sample collection letters that can be modified to meet your needs. They are professional and contain all the information needed. Note that neither letter is accusatory in nature, nor does either ask for anything other than the prompt payment of monies owed.

Sample Collection Letter #1

(Insert date)
(Insert name and address)

Dear _____,

   It was a pleasure speaking with you today regarding invoice no. ######, dated xx/xx/xxxx, in the amount of $x, xxx.00. I just want to confirm that this invoice will be paid on xx/xx/xxxx, as you stated in our phone conversation.

   I am enclosing a copy of this invoice for your reference. Should there be any reason this invoice cannot be paid as stated above, please contact me immediately.

Sincerely,

Name
Phone number
E-mail address

Sample Collection Letter #2

(Insert date)
(Insert name and address)

Dear _____,

In accordance with our telephone conversation today I would like to confirm that invoice no. xxxxx, dated xx/xx/xxxx in the amount of $x, xxx.00, will be paid on xx/xx/xxxx. If you recall, in our conversation of xx/xx/xxxx, you stated that this invoice was scheduled for payment on xx/xx/xxxx. Since payment has not yet been received, we are understandably concerned. A company's credit rating is a very valuable asset and something we do our best to help our customers maintain.

I am enclosing a copy of this invoice for your reference. Should there be any reason this invoice cannot be paid as stated above, please contact me immediately to prevent any further action.

Sincerely,

Name
Phone number
E-mail address

Understanding Insurance

Business insurance can be a very complicated issue. It is the one product that you purchase with the intent of never using it. Many different types of business insurance are available today. With the increasing complexity of today's business environment, it is impossible to become an expert in all these different types of insurance, so it is extremely important to obtain your insurance through a trusted insurance agency. You will depend greatly on the experience and expertise of your agency to guide you through the maze of insurance products and issues.

Below is a list of the basic types of business insurance available, along with a short description of the type of coverage for each product.

1. Directors and Officers insurance is designed to provide liability protection to the individual officers and directors of a small business or corporation beyond the coverage the corporation itself may provide to protect them from lawsuits or judgments against their personal property that arise from their activities for the company or management decisions made on behalf of the company.
2. General Liability insurance protects the company against liability claims from outside sources for accidents, injuries, or damages that

may occur on the company's premises or be caused by the company's products or processes.
3. Garage Keepers insurance protects a corporation with customer's vehicles on their property against liability claims from damage to those customer vehicles.
4. Health Care insurance provides a certain degree of protection for the insured employee against specific medical related costs. It is very complex and has been made more so by the Affordable Care Act.
5. Worker's Compensation insurance provides coverage for employees for any medical related costs, wages, and disabilities that result from an injury incurred in the performance of an employee's duties in the workplace. It is generally mandated by the state in which the company operates. Payment is based on each individual state's worker's compensation laws.
6. Pollution insurance provides liability coverage for site cleanup and restoration following accidental spills or other types of environmental mishaps, as defined in the policy. It is generally very specific and limited to this effect on the environment. It can provide some degree of coverage for cleanup and restoration costs that result from an accident occurring on the company's property. This policy may or may not cover cleanup, products, or off- or on-site transportation. Coverage is individual, based on the way the policy is written.
7. Employment Practices insurance provides liability coverage for errors in the human resource practices and policies of the company. It generally does not provide any coverage for violation of any federal, state, or local laws or violation of any employee's rights of employment.
8. Commercial Property insurance covers the physical property the company owns and is one of the most common types of insurance available to a company with physical assets.
9. Professional Liability insurance, also known as errors and omissions insurance, covers professionals in the performance of their

profession. Lawyers, doctors, and accountants, for example, generally all carry some type of professional liability insurance.
10. Umbrella policy is a type of liability insurance, an additive product that provides additional coverage on top of other specific coverage. It is basically a low-cost way of providing extra insurance coverage once the specific insurance product has reached its maximum limit.
11. Crime policy protects the company from dishonest acts committed by employees that result in a loss of company assets, including money and securities, and covers embezzlement, forgery, wire transfer fraud, burglary, and robbery.

Although this is a list of the common types of business insurance available, it is by no means a complete list. Bear in mind that each type of insurance includes a long list of exclusions. You must pay close attention to those exclusions in order to fully understand your insurance coverage.

It is very common for an insured company or individual to believe he or she has full coverage for foreseeable events only to find out when filing a claim that there is an applicable exclusion clause in the coverage. These exclusion clauses cause a great deal of anxiety when claims are being filed.

Most insurance companies or agencies now have educational programs to help you keep your claims at a minimum and lower your premiums. These programs include understanding human resources administration, good safety practices, and the fundamentals of healthcare insurance, among others. With the ever-increasing cost of insurance, it is certainly important to take advantage of all of these educational opportunities to ensure you get all the insurance you need.

One of the most valuable opportunities to reduce insurance costs is control of the work environment to keep employees safe. While it costs very little to insure office workers against Workers Compensation claims, it costs a great deal more to insure mechanics or roofers in the performance of their duties. It's generally worth the time and effort to develop and implement a comprehensive and effective safety program, which can yield benefits not only to the company but also to the individual employee.

I find it very valuable to continue to shop and compare insurance policies and not assume that the insurance coverage and premiums you currently have are the best and most affordable. It is essential to push your insurance providers to give you the best deal they possibly can. Having said that, it is just as critical to establish and maintain a close relationship with your insurance agency.

Your insurance agency will fight on your behalf when you have any disputes with insurance carriers. The agency does not underwrite the insurance policies; it simply sells and administers the policies. The willingness of the agency to speak to the insurance carrier on your behalf, when a claim has been filed, is vital to your ability to receive and maintain needed coverage. Do not underestimate the value of your local insurance agency or agencies. They can be critical partners exactly when you need them most.

A Guide to Planning

> "Before beginning, prepare carefully."
> —Marcus Tullius Cicero
> Roman Statesman
> 1st Century BC

As you can see from the above quotation, the importance of planning for your own success was well known over two thousand years ago. In fact, nearly all great generals, civic leaders and business leaders have well understood the role careful planning has in the success of a person or an organization. Planning is preparation for success.

Running a business without proper planning is often compared to driving across the country without a map or in the absence of any road signs. I have found this to be an accurate assessment. Planning will show you the best way to get to your destination.

Why Planning Is Critical

Planning can show you what needs to be done. It is the most essential tool you have in making your future what you would like it to be. It is also the most critical aspect of managing a successful business. If you need to raise money, a good business plan can help you do that: you can use it to show potential investors why they should invest in your company, or why bankers should lend you money. It is sometimes required by vendors who are thinking about extending significant credit to your business. If you don't plan for the success of your business, you will get exactly what you planned for.

Planning Can Be Difficult

Although planning is critical to your success, it is often overlooked in favor of intuition or "gut feeling." Other obstacles also hinder planning, including:

- Lack of know-how—it is sometimes difficult to know how to plan or what to plan for.
- Fear of the unknown—it is hard enough dealing with the problems of today without worrying about what's going to happen in the future.
- Inexactness—since even the best plans do not always work out as they were intended, it can be perceived as an exercise in futility.

These obstacles are very real. However, they must be overcome if you are to be successful. It is much more problematic to face the future without a plan than it is to face the future with a plan. So let's address the plan for business success.

The first plan you should make is your exit-strategy plan. Whether you own your business outright or are managing a business, you should have an exit-strategy plan. That is, you need to know how you plan to quit the business. Do you intend to sell your company and retire? Are you planning to leave your business to someone in your family? If so, do you plan to mentor your replacement? Looked at in this light, all other business planning then becomes a part of your long-term exit-strategy plan.

What Is a Business Plan?

"Our goals can only be reached through a vehicle of a plan, in which we fervently believe, and upon which we must vigorously act."

—Pablo Picasso
Spanish Artist
1881-1973

A business plan is a written document that clearly defines the goals of a business and outlines the methods for achieving those goals. It describes what a business does, how it will be done, who has to do it, where it will be done, why it's being done, and when it has to be done. Business plans are too important to be ignored.

Dreams and ambitions are great and important, but results are what really count in the business world. Therefore, it is important to establish realistic goals along with a sound methodology for achieving them.

There are basically two types of business plans—operational and financial. The type of plan that you create will depend upon its purpose. If you are writing a business plan to seek investment, it must be more extensive and descriptive in nature than an ongoing business plan, which is your guide to future success. I have written business plans that are long and extensive as well as business plans that are short and to the point. One is not necessarily better than the other and one will not necessarily ensure greater success than the other. As long as your business plan is a written description of how you will achieve the success you are striving for, the form or the length of the plan really does not matter. Here are some key characteristics of a successful business plan.

- It is the management and financial guide for a successful business.
- It is written by the management team.
- It is realistic and executable.

- It explains how the business will function and describes its operations.
- It details how the business will be capitalized (in the case of a start-up business).

Elements of a Business Plan

No matter how formal or informal your business plan may be it should consist of the following elements. There should be a brief description of your business as well as a description of the products and services it offers. There should also be a section on sales and marketing and, finally, a section on financial management. If you are writing a business plan to raise capital, these essential elements should be extensive enough to ensure that the reader understands your business. This is critical if you are, for example, trying to get a bank loan. Let's go over these elements in greater detail.

A formal business plan must start with a description of your business, including not only a physical description, but also a general description of the industry. Take the time to carefully consider your business and your industry. This is your opportunity to take a thirty-thousand-foot view of the industry, which often yields some insights into changes that will be necessary for your company to succeed. Busy executives often do not take the time to take this higher-level view of the company. They allow themselves to get overloaded by the daily running of the business and can lose perspective of the overall plan. Creating a general description of your business can afford you the opportunity to regain that perspective.

Products and Services

The second section of a formal business should be a description of products and services. This could be as long and detailed or as short as necessary to fully explain what products or services your company offers. Again, this is an opportunity to analyze your company's operations and make note of any changes that will be needed as you move forward. By taking a close look at what your company is offering, you can sometimes see the weaknesses in your product offering and turn those weaknesses into opportunities.

Sales and Marketing

Sales and marketing are often considered to be the core of any business, as this is where you show how the business will successfully generate revenue. In doing so, you must differentiate your company from your competition. This takes careful analysis and requires you to be honest in your assessment of your company's strengths and weaknesses. Understanding your strengths and weaknesses allows you to clearly see your business opportunities and any threats against those opportunities.

A more complete description of the sales and marketing function of your business is contained in the sales and marketing chapter. We will look carefully at the essential aspects of sales and marketing in that chapter, so here we will only deal with the components of a sales and marketing plan.

Sales and marketing plans must address several key questions:

- What are your products or services?
- Who are your customers, and how large is the market?
- Who is your competition, and how will you successfully compete against them?
- What is your pricing structure? Will it be on the high end or on the low end of the market?
- Will you sell your products and services directly to your customers or through distribution channels?

An extensive sales and marketing plan is essential to your long-term success. Because the plan is so critical and can be very extensive, we will continue this topic in the chapter on Marketing.

Financial Management

The financial management section is often considered the most critical part of your business plan. That is certainly true for a business start-up seeking financing. We have already discussed financial matters in previous chapters, so we will not do that again here. Please refer to those chapters for a greater understanding of financial management. The business plan, though, must include the key elements of financial management:

- Income statements and balance sheets for the past two years (if available)
- Projected income statements and balance sheets for the next two years
- Projected cash-flow statement for twelve months

Is critical that you include an explanation of any and all projections, especially if you're a start-up company seeking financing. The bottom line is that you must clearly show how your company will make a profit. This is what investors and banks want to know.

Goal Setting

Planning is a critical part of running a successful business. If you run a business without a plan, even a successful business, you just take what you get without understanding the reasons for your success—or failure.

"A goal without a plan is just a wish!"

— Antoine de Saint-Exupery
French Novelist
1900 - 1944

Following are two goal-setting guides that I have found useful in the planning process. The first is simply a general template for goal setting. This simple worksheet makes clear that goal setting is a process and walks you through the process step by step. You may want to use it to guide you through the process of making sure your business goals are identified, executable, and achievable.

The second guide will help ensure that your personal goals and the goals for your business are compatible. The key to completing this guide is to first complete the section on personal goals and then wait two or three days to complete the section on business goals, without referring back to the section on personal goals. Only after completing both sections should you compare the two. You are looking for any conflicts between personal and business goals. I have used both of these guides extensively.

Goal-Setting Template
(One worksheet per goal)
Goal (Be specific)
_____
_____

Measurement (The bench mark that tells you that you have achieved the goal)
_____

Strategies to achieve goal (The overall means of achieving your stated goal)
1)_____

2)_____

3)_____
_____

Tactics/Actions (Must support strategies—be specific and include a deadline)

What—_____
_____
When—_____
Who—_____

What—_____
_____
When—_____
Who—_____

What—_____
_____
When—_____
Who—_____

What—_____
_____
When—_____
Who—_____

Direct costs of executing tactics

Tactic #_____Cost in $_____
Tactic #_____Cost in $_____
Tactic #_____Cost in $_____
Tactic #_____Cost in $_____
Tactic #_____Cost in $_____

Personal Goals Template
(Complete this section before the section on business goals.)

What do you want to change or what difference would you like to see in your personal life? How will you accomplish this?

Goals for the Next Twelve Months

1. _____
2. _____
3. _____
4. _____

Actions (to be) Taken   Cost

1. _____   _____
2. _____   _____
3. _____   _____
4. _____   _____

Goals for the Next One to Three Years

1. _____
2. _____
3. _____
4. _____

Actions (to be) Taken   Cost

1. _____   _____
2. _____   _____
3. _____   _____
4. _____   _____

Business Goals Template

(Complete two to three days after the section on personal goals and without referring back to that section.)

What do you want to change or what difference do you want to see in your business?
_____

How will you accomplish this?
_____

Goals for the Next Twelve Months

1. _____
2. _____
3. _____
4. _____

Actions (to be) Taken	Cost
1. _____	_____
2. _____	_____
3. _____	_____
4. _____	_____

Goals for the Next One to Three Years

1. _____
2. _____
3. _____
4. _____

Actions (to be) Taken   Cost

1. _____   _____
2. _____   _____
3. _____   _____
4. _____   _____

Thoughts and comments on any conflicts between personal goals and business goals.

_____
_____
_____

Good planning begets good performance. A lack of planning or poor planning leaves you wondering what happened and why. We all want to be successful. The question is, are you willing to plan for that success or do you just hope it comes to you by some stroke of luck?

It is also important to realize that all plans are constantly in need of updating. A plan you wrote a year ago is in danger of being outdated. Situations change, competitors come and go, new products are introduced. I recommend that you update your business plans at least every year, although every six months is even better.

"It is a bad plan that admits no modification."

—Publilius Syrus
Latin Writer
1st Century BC

The Budgeting Process

In its most basic form, budgeting is a part of planning for success. It is a tool for dealing with the future. It helps you understand how you can turn your wishes into reality. It is imperative that you think of budgeting as a process. It is never a project with an endpoint. The process helps you to determine how you can attain your profitability goals. An increase in profit (or decrease in loss) should be your first consideration when you think about the budget for the next year and beyond.

Done correctly, the budgeting process will help you answer some very important questions.

- What sales will be needed to meet your profit goals?
- What expenses will be necessary to support those sales, and is there anything that can be done to lower those expenses?
- What gross margin can you achieve, and is that margin sufficient to achieve your desired profitability?
- Is an improvement in revenue solely a result of improving the sales process, or are other factors involved, such as improving customer service?

These are just a few questions that can be answered in the budgeting process.

Benjamin Franklin is credited with saying, "The only things certain in life are death and taxes!" I believe that the failure to plan for success (to budget) will almost certainly result in the death of the business. The only question is how long that death will take. It is also certain that if you operate a profitable business you will pay taxes. So, this Franklin quote has ongoing relevance to business.

The business environment is fluid, and all businesses must operate in that fluid environment. Not much in the business world, beyond death and taxes, is etched in stone. Because business is not stagnant, the budget process can often uncover problems and present choices. The more you work on budgeting, the more you come to understand what changes are occurring and what choices you have to meet those changes.

Too many managers run their businesses without a plan, simply trying to survive from month to month. Those managers overlook an important management tool: budgeting. Think of budgeting as a road map showing how you will get from point A to point B. How challenging would it be to drive from New York City to Los Angeles if there were no maps, no GPS, and there were no road signs? It would be difficult at best. So, let's look at the fundamentals of budgeting.

The Fundamentals of Budgeting

A budget is in reality a projected profit and loss statement and a resultant balance sheet based on a specific set of assumptions. It is a detailed plan of future receipts and expenditures, which either result in a profit or a loss. Since a budget is a projected profit and loss statement, it allows you to compare your budget projections with actual results. You may find that your revenue projections were very good, but that your expense projections were not. If your expenses were higher than expected, you would look for ways to lower them. Conversely, if your revenue fell short, you would look for methods to increase revenue.

The budgeting process can either be top down or bottom up. In a top down process, you start with the revenue line and work down through COGS and expenses to arrive at a projected profit. In the bottom up process, you start with your desired profit and work backward until you project the revenue you need to support your desired profit. Most large businesses use the latter method. In other words, they decide what profit they want to make and then list the expenses and COGS that they will incur and the revenue they need in order to make that predetermined profit.

I have found this method to be fraught with pitfalls that often result in a failure to make the revenue numbers. You can exert direct, but not total, control over expenses. You can only impact revenue. You cannot control it. If you need verification that bottom up budgeting is very challenging, look at how often large companies are battered on Wall Street after missing their revenue projections. Remember, they do not purposely miss their revenue projections. They simply fail to understand the basic principle that while they can control costs, they can only influence revenue. Remember Blackberry Z10, the supposed iPhone killer. Blackberry reportedly lost over one billion dollars on that product launch.

The budget process starts with analyzing your current operations and realized profitability. You need to have sufficient profitability to retire any debt and provide a reasonable return to the ownership. It is not uncommon for an owner of a small business to actually make less from profits than he or she would make simply being an employee of another company. This is especially true in the service industry where a busy plumber or electrician can easily earn more working for someone else than working on his or her own. In this case, profitability is viewed against other available alternatives. Profitability must also provide sufficient funds to reinvest in the company's future.

Now that you have a place to start, you can begin planning for next year's budget. Experience has shown me that most companies do a better job of top down budgeting than bottom up budgeting. You must decide which methodology to use. I prefer to start at the revenue line, not the profit line.

To begin, look at your revenue for the current year and use that to project future revenue. The key is to be both optimistic and realistic at the same time. After all, it does no good to make revenue projections that look good on paper but are simply not attainable in the real world.

Any revenue projection should be a stretch, but make it an achievable stretch. This will force you and your team to continually do the thousands of things necessary to reach the revenue goal. If you are continuing with the same products and services you currently have, then be realistic about your company's ability to increase revenue year after year.

Remember, for revenue to increase without new products or services, you will most likely need to increase your market share. Without an expanding market (for example, cell phones), it is a real challenge for any company to increase its market share without adding products or services. So, ask yourself how you are going to increase revenue. Will you add new products? Will you call on a new set of potential customers? Will you improve your customer service?

Reaching the Goal

Once you have decided on your revenue goals, you can now focus your attention to COGS. Effective management of the costs of goods sold is perhaps the most viable opportunity for profit generation. Why is that? Because your production costs are usually the largest costs any company incurs. Let's face it, labor is expensive. To waste labor on nonproductive tasks or to underutilize labor increases your labor costs and therefore leaves you with a smaller margin. Remember, your margin is your total revenue less all costs directly attributable to generating that revenue.

Remember also that margin is the ultimate driver of profits. The larger the margin, the more you have left to cover overhead and provide for profitability. To do this, you must project your future COGS as a percentage of future revenue. The good news is that you should already have this percentage available from your previous profit and loss statements. This is your starting point. Improving that margin percentage is a solid business goal.

Once you have projected your margin, you can move on to projecting overhead. Overhead consists of both fixed and variable expenses. Fixed expenses are expenses such as rent and insurance. Variable expenses are expenses such as utilities and supplies. Again, these expenses are readily available to you from your profit and loss statement. In analyzing expenses, think carefully about whether you can make any quick and significant changes to ongoing expenses. Be vigilant, diligent, and realistic in looking at expenses.

If you need to add people to your business, then you must account for that in your budget. Adding a new phone system? Put it in the budget. Upgrading your IT abilities? Put it in the budget. A manager's need and desire to do things that increase expenses must be part of the budget process.

Too many times I have seen a manager spend significant money on a necessary, but unbudgeted, item only to ask at a later date, "Why are expenses so high?" Of course the answer is that those expenditures were not in the budget. Everyone must make course corrections. They are part of the reality of business. But you need to forecast as much as you can in order to avoid unpleasant surprises.

Most accounting packages export accurate reports, providing the information you input is accurate. Without accurate numbers you are not planning, you are guessing. Spend the time to make sure revenue and expense items are accurately recorded. This is particularly important in deciding whether an item belongs in COGS or overhead. Costs of goods sold are those costs directly associated with the generation of revenue. Overhead expenses are other costs (e.g., electricity, insurance). Don't fixate, but do strive for accuracy.

Trends

It is most helpful to look at both revenue and expense items in terms of trends. When analyzing the income statement, I always convert each COGS line and each overhead line to a percentage of revenue, to easily compare this year's performance to last year's performance. Converting each line item to a revenue percentage allows you to compare apples to apples in earlier periods. Comparing each period's performance to that of prior periods, you can spot trends. It is the trend that tells the story, not any specific month or quarter.

Comparing your current trends to your budgeted numbers is also useful and allows you to catch a developing problem before it becomes serious. Such diligence allows you to keep small problems from becoming big problems.

Bottom Line

It is important to keep in mind that the budgeting process is not just an attempt to put numbers together for next year's operations. A properly done budget forces you to analyze your current operations as well as to look forward to future operations. Part of the budgeting process is an extensive analysis of how your company is currently operating. By comparing your current period's operating numbers to those of previous periods, you can easily spot the trends that need to be addressed.

I once had a business owner say to me that he never budgets because he has no idea what the future will bring. This is an inherently weak working philosophy, and I believe it is one of the reasons why he never was able to grow his business beyond organic growth. (Think or organic growth as the rate of growth your company would have if you did nothing to try and increase revenue.) It is also true that many business owners look at budgeting the same way they look at cash flow. That is to say, they look at money in the bank account and use that as a budget. This, of course, is not a budget. It is just a number.

Below is an example of a simple budget. It compares budgeted numbers to actual numbers, which allows you to focus on any problem areas. This budget is for demonstration purposes only, but this is how budgets really work. This type of analysis is critical to understanding and then positively affecting company performance.

(Fiscal Year 20xx)

	Budget	Actual	Difference	%
REVENUE				
Revenue Category 1	90000	91000	1000	101%
Revenue Category 2	80000	81000	1000	101%
Revenue Category 3	70000	71000	1000	101%
Total Income	240000	243000	3000	101%
COGS				
Labor Category 1	25000	24000	-1000	96%
Labor Category 2	20000	19000	-1000	95%
Materials Category 1	25000	24000	-1000	96%
Materials Category 2	20000	19000	-1000	95%
Other COGS	25000	24000	-1000	96%
Total COGS	115000	110000	-5000	96%
Gross Margin	125000	133000	8000	106%
Gross Margin Percentage	52%	55%	3%	
OVERHEAD EXPENSES				
Salaries	40000	40000	0	100%
Other Payroll Expense	1000	1000	0	100%
Paid Time Off	4000	3500	500	88%
Payroll taxes	4000	3500	500	88%
Workers Comp	10000	9000	1000	90%
Benefits	5000	4900	100	98%
Repairs	10000	9500	500	95%
Office Supplies	2500	2300	200	92%
Fuel	2500	2300	200	92%
Insurance	6000	5500	500	92%
Taxes	1000	1000	0	100%
Advertising	2000	2500	-500	125%
Other Miscellaneous	2000	1800	200	90%
All utilities	5000	6000	-1000	120%
Professional Services	1000	800	200	80%
Total Expenses	96000	93600	2400	98%
Net Operating Income	29000	39400	10400	136%
Interest Expense	2000	2000	0	100%
Depreciation	3000	3000	0	100%
Other Expenses	1000	1000	0	100%
Net Profit	23000	33400	10400	145%

In analyzing this budget, a few things stand out. First, the company is exceeding its budgeted revenue goal by 1 percent. That's good. Second, it is 4 percent under budget on its COGS. This is also good. When you combine the excess in budgeted revenue with the under budgeted COGS, the company has exceeded its budgeted gross margin by 6 percent. That is the key factor in this budget.

Since the company has also managed to control its expenses and is actually 2 percent under budgeted expense numbers, the company posts a net operating profit that exceeds the budget by 36 percent. This is where you can see that a small increase in revenue and a small decrease in COGS percentage coupled with a small decrease in budgeted expenses all combine to yield a fairly large percentage increase in net operating profit. This is the leverage effect of combining small gains in each area to achieve markedly strong results.

Much can be gained by budgeting. To be an effective manager, proper diligence must be applied to the budgeting process in order to move your company forward. You either budget for success or you fail to do so and take what you get. There is an old saying that remains as viable today as it was many years ago.

"He who fails to plan, plans to fail."
— Proverb

Forecasting Sales

Sales forecasting is the process of organizing and analyzing information so as to estimate what your sales will be in a future time period with a reasonable degree of confidence. Sales revenues from the current year make a good starting point for predicting sales in the following year. For example, if the trend in the general economy is a growth of 5 percent for next year, it may be entirely acceptable for you to forecast next year's sales at 5 percent higher than your actual sales in the current year. However, the general economic climate is only one part of the equation.

You must also look at your specific industry, your company offering and current market position, your competition, and the strategies you are implementing to grow revenue. Only by taking into account all of these factors can you produce a forecast that has a reasonable chance of success.

You need a sales forecast before you can create a company budget. It is the essential element in the revenue portion of the budget and is closely tied to the company's gross margin. You cannot forecast sales without understanding how the desired gross margin percentage affects sales volume. Since gross margin percentages are determined by a combination of pricing policy and production efficiency, it is important to understand how this relationship affects sales volume.

All other things being equal, an increase in desired gross margin, which results from an increase in pricing, will usually have some effect on sales volume. A decision to increase the expected gross margin percentage, by raising prices, may decrease expected sales. Conversely, reducing the expected gross profit percentages by price reductions may increase sales. (This is basic pricing theory. In reality it is almost never that simple.) I will further address gross margin percentages shortly.

A second major reason for beginning the budget process with the sales forecast is that sales volume often impacts expenses. Here are some items that may be impacted by changes in sales volume:

- Variable expenses, which could include expenses such as sales commissions, sales support functions, additional support personnel, or delivery costs.
- Various fixed costs, even though these expenses normally do not vary directly with sales volume. Over the long run there may be significant effects, as an increase in sales volume may give rise to the need for additional office space or warehouse space, a bookkeeping department or a collections department.
- Capital expenditures might rise, such as for plant expansion or additional vehicles.
- Working capital accounts could change as a result of borrowing for expansion.

Realism

A realistic sales forecast must rely on careful analysis of market potential and the ability of your business to capture its share of that potential. The forecast should be based on what you can do rather than on what you hope to do. The first approach is analytical and realistic, while the other is wishful.

The realistic approach dictates that an increase in forecasted sales must result from changes you are making in your company, from an increase in demand in your industry, or some combination of both. Anyone selling cell phones in the last twenty years has seen a tremendous increase in demand across the industry. It follows that sales volume should also increase. Just look at AT&T, Verizon, or T-Mobile for proof of this concept.

Conversely, if you were in almost any brick-and-mortar business in the last twenty years, you have most likely lost revenue to online businesses. Remember, any forecast of a sales increase must be realistic and supportable. The concept, "If I build it they will come," is not realistic and should not form the basis for a sales forecast.

As stated earlier, the sales forecast will be a driving force in many important decisions you will have to make. Therefore accuracy, based on real world conditions, is paramount. You might be trying to decide whether or not to expand. If you do decide to expand, will that be a physical expansion? Will the expansion be of personnel only? Will you need to secure financing for that expansion?

The goal here is to be ready for the future without wasting valuable resources. Remember, both lenders and potential investors will look at your revenue forecasts in their decision-making. As computer programmers have always said, "Garbage in, garbage out!"

Any sales forecast that is greater than the expansion rate for the general economy requires a detailed plan for achieving its targets. This is where your marketing plan is critical—we will look at a marketing plan, in detail, in a later chapter. Marketing information should include an analysis of the industry, of your company, and of your customer's needs, along with a plan to address those needs. You may be looking to introduce new products or services or to expand in completely new markets. All of these factors feed into the sales forecast and should be carefully considered in your plan. Your plan must contain specific actions that can be taken to achieve the results projected in your sales forecast.

Revenue Categories

Your sales forecast will begin with an analysis of your current company performance and will most likely be divided into categories by revenue line. Your company may provide products and services in several different categories. You may be in the roofing business, for example, and therefore have a revenue line for new roofs, one for roof repairs, for guttering, and for any other goods or services you may provide. Retail stores generally categorize sales by selling department. Department store chains generally categorize sales by store or region. Insurance brokerage firms generally categorize revenue by type of insurance product.

Revenue, in most businesses, is easy to categorize and analyze individually. The categories used will depend upon the nature of your business.

Sales-Influencing Factors

In any business various factors affect sales. As you review the revenue categories for your business, you must take into account the factors that will either positively or negatively impact revenue in each category. Some of these factors are internal, and some are external. Internal factors are items that you have direct control or considerable influence over. External factors are items over which you generally have very little control. All must be considered by category. Here are some of the factors that might influence your sales forecast:

Internal Factors

- Marketing plans
- Capacity expansion plans

- New products
- Pricing policy
- Sales force expansion

External Factors

- General economy
- Government policies or programs
- Inflation
- Weather
- Purchased products
- Competition

Gross Margin Percentages

Before finalizing revenue projections, make sure you take a look at your company's gross margin percentage. You do not want to leave any money on the table, but you also do not want to set your gross margin so high that it negatively impacts revenue. As stated above, you may be able to directly impact internal costs (hourly wage rate, production efficiency, etc.) but you may have very little impact on the cost of products purchased.

Unless you are purchasing very large quantities of an item (as Walmart does), your influence over the cost of what you purchase will be limited. However, an examination of your current percentages will give you a good indication of both your pricing policy and your production efficiency. Are you really getting the best pricing from your vendors, or are you just purchasing from the same vendors you have always used? Take a look; the result may surprise you.

The gross margin percentages should also be compared to those of prior years and to your objectives for the current year to compare how well you're meeting the goals you have set for your company. Assuming that the goals you have set are realistic, the gross margin percentage is often the most critical factor in determining ultimate profitability. In comparing gross margins over time, you are looking for significant variations from your projections, which should be quickly addressed.

If at all possible, it is very helpful to look at your gross margin percentages and compare them against an industry average. This may not be possible, as the information may not be readily available. Whenever comparison is possible, it can provide valuable insight to for your internal operations.

Do not be fooled by the common excuse that your business is so different from everyone else's that this comparison is not valid. It is. This is an opportunity for improvement that will be lost if you adopt the attitude that your business is unique and cannot be compared to other businesses. A far more productive attitude is to ask, "If everyone else is getting a higher gross margin than we are getting, what do we need to do to improve our margin?" You should make every attempt possible to bring your performance in line with industry averages, at a minimum. If you cannot do so, ask why not. Be specific in your answer.

It is important to compare your current operating margin with margins from prior periods, at least monthly, to understand current operating trends and to identify needed changes. I recommend not only comparing gross margins for current and prior periods, but also doing so for all of your expenses to prior period's expenses. This is easily accomplished by converting each expense line to a percentage of revenue, which will allow you to easily see whether your expenses are increasing or decreasing, with regard to revenue, over time.

Conclusions

Comparing gross margin with the industry averages (if available) or with prior periods should raise important questions. Here are some questions to keep you focused:

- Would a more competitive pricing structure allow you to capture a larger market share?
- If capturing a larger market share would require giving up gross margin, should you do so? (The answer this question may be "Yes" or "No" depending upon the goals of the company.)
- Are you making the most effective purchasing decisions?
- Are you significantly underpricing your product?
- Are your salespeople cutting prices to gain revenue but, in the process of doing so, losing gross margin?
- Is your marketing plan correctly focused on high margin items? If not, why not?
- Is too much of your marketing effort focused on a few large volume customers?

Your sales forecast is both complicated and critical to your overall success. Time must be spent on understanding the variables in your forecast. Consideration must be paid to your pricing structure, your gross margin, industry trends, customer needs, and so forth. It is important to revise your sales forecast as needed to meet your operating goals.

Any sales forecast should be optimistic in nature. However, realism is essential in making plans for operational success. It is as important to not underestimate your sales revenue, as it is to not overestimate your sales revenue. By asking the right questions and understanding the effects of the answers to those questions on your business, you will put yourself in a much better position to achieve your goals.

Marketing Your Company

Marketing is both persuasive and informational. An effective marketing program will influence purchasing behavior by influencing the thought patterns of your target audience. The influencing of thought patterns is done by projecting your company image as being the best choice your customers could make in deciding with whom they want to do business.

All customers in the marketplace are constantly in this decision-making process. It is not a one-time decision or an event that has an endpoint. This is an ongoing process in which you constantly tell the story of why it is in the best interest of your customers and your targets to do business with you.

Marketing is typically targeted toward the acquisition of new customers. Most business owners believe that if they could just get a few more customers their lives would be good. While every business wants new customers, an effective marketing campaign must always take into consideration the retention of current customers. It costs very little to retain current customers. It is much more expensive to get new customers. Look at Walmart. Their marketing is not just aimed at new customers. They are constantly reminding their current customer base that they are saving money and have a great selection when they shop at Walmart.

Start looking at your marketing program by analyzing your current situation. Look at your own company before you look at anything else. If you are not getting the results you want, look in the mirror first.

Company Analysis

The best place to start when trying to understand your current marketing situation is with an analysis of your company. You want to know your strengths and your weaknesses and thereby understand the opportunities for improvement available to you. Sometimes this can be very difficult to do. It is certainly not unusual for a business owner or manager to see his or her company much differently than others, outside the company, would see it. This is most especially true for small businesses where the owner has put in a tremendous amount of blood, sweat, and tears to build up the company. My experience has been that owners not only often have a skewed vision of how the company operates, but also misjudge the company's position in the marketplace. This is not done intentionally; it simply results from wishful thinking.

In analyzing your company's position, you must look at not only top-level management but management at all levels. Some managers will perform excellently, and others will not. This is also true of employees who are not in management. Carefully looking at your company's personnel capabilities helps you not only understand what you are currently able to do well, but also what changes must be made as you move forward.

A critical part of analyzing your company is an understanding of the image a company projects in the marketplace. Is your company a high-priced, high-service company, such as Lexus, or a low-priced warehouse-type operation, such as Costco? Both of these approaches have proven to be successful in the marketplace, but they are very different from an operational standpoint. Obviously, both Lexus and Costco operate very profitably and are leaders in their field. Lexus does so with high-priced products and Costco with low-priced products. What is critical to understand then, is your company image and its proper positioning in your market. Here are some of the questions you should ask in doing a company analysis:

- What products or services do you offer?
- What are your company's strengths and weaknesses? (It is important to be honest about both.)
- Do you have the right management team (with the right experience, talents, and skills)?
- Are you providing your employees the tools they need to excel?
- What is the company image (quality at a high price—Lexus—or low-price big retailer—Costco)?
- What is the value proposition behind your company (why should someone do business with you)?

Before you can know how to win over new customers, you must first know yourself. This analysis can only be of help in making decisions that affect your future.

Once you have analyzed your company, analyze your customers.

Customer Analysis

A customer analysis is generally straightforward and can provide insights into expansion opportunities. Start by looking at your current customer base as if you were an outsider to the company. How can you best describe that customer base in terms that you can then use in a marketing program? In looking at customers from an outsider's standpoint, you may see that your customer base is not as homogenous as you think.

Remember that customers come in all shapes and sizes. You need to look at your customers' income levels as well as their buying habits. If you are Lexus automobile dealership, your customer base probably looks very different from the customer base of a Ford dealership, even though both dealerships sell cars. There may be differences in education levels, income levels, and lifestyles as well as in the customers' own perceptions of what is important to them. Remember, there is no right or wrong here, no good or bad. There are only differences that you must take into account when creating your marketing plan.

You should always consider how you could expand your customer base. What additional products or services could you offer that would bring in a whole new customer base? Consider Apple computers, for example. The company started out as a personal-computer company that later expanded its product offering into the music and personal-electronics market, very successfully, which has given it much greater opportunities than it had prior to the expansion. Apple's customer base is now much larger and more expansive in its scope than it was when it was simply selling computers. It is now selling its products to a much younger market demographic than previously.

The electronics market is continuing to expand, and people are using iPhones, iPods, and iPads at ever-younger ages. It certainly is not unusual to see adolescents as young as twelve or thirteen with their own cell phones. This expanded revenue stream would not have been available to Apple had it limited its offering to the personal-computer market.

Although the analysis of your customer base may seem fairly easy, do not fall into the trap of believing that the customer base is unchangeable. In fact it is very changeable, based upon new products or services you may wish to offer. Whether or not these changes in the product offering are viable is a question you must ask as you go through the process of deciding whether or not to expand your product line. In looking at your customers, here are some questions you should ask:

- Who are your primary customers, and what are they like? (Be descriptive and objective.)

- What are your target market constraints? (Geographic, income, age, etc.)
- Why do your current customers buy your product or service? (The primary reason.)
- How can you encourage them to buy more of your product or service?
- How would you best describe potential customers with whom you do not currently do business?
- What do potential customers need most from you?

A full and accurate picture of your customer base is important for making future plans and decisions. It is always important to "dance with the one who brought you"—do not ignore the potential for additional revenue from your current customer base. But it is also important to keep your eyes open and your head on a swivel to look out for other potential dance partners!

Competition

Competition is a fact and a by-product of a free market. Almost all companies face it. In a free market, competition can drive down pricing and can force improvements in efficiency. In that sense, it is seen as a good thing. Even though every business owner would love to be in a market free of competition, it's not going to happen. So, knowing your competition is important. In fact, it is vital.

It is generally impractical to look in detail at every competitor you may have. Frequently, though, some of your competition does not have a strong effect on your company. This allows you to focus your attention on your strong competitors, looking for their strengths and weaknesses. You need to know their pricing structure, their management abilities, their products and services, and how you may be losing customers to them. This information is vital to knowing how you can effectively take market share from them. Remember, it is all about slicing up the pie; if your industry is not expanding (and the pie is not getting bigger), you can only expand by getting yourself a bigger piece of that pie.

In devising your competitive strategies, you should assume that 1) your competition is not going away; and 2) if you are not trying to take market share from them, you will most likely lose market share to them. If your competition is smart, then they are doing the same analysis of your company that you are doing of theirs.

Do not fear your competition, but do respect their capabilities. Try to learn something from them. Undoubtedly they do some things better than you, and you do some things better than them. Knowing what they do better, and why, is the first step to improving your competitive position. To gain market share, you must take customers from your competitors. That is simply the world in which we live. Here are some basic questions regarding your competition that need answers:

- Who are your major competitors?
- What are their strengths and weaknesses?
- Why do customers buy their product or service? (What is their competitive advantage?)
- Is their share of the market increasing or decreasing, and why?
- What do their strengths tell you about where you must improve?

Finally, always treat your competition with the greatest respect. Disdain for your competition usually leads to losing customers to them. If your company is doing well and they are still competing against you, they too must be doing something right!

Pricing Structure

The pricing of your goods and services helps to define your company image and will relay important information to your customers and potential customers. We all understand the pricing differences between a Lexus automobile and a Ford; it speaks to us about the assumed differences in the quality of the product being purchased as well as the level of service after the sale.

It is not always true that the difference in the actual quality of a product is reflected in the difference in pricing. However, the perception remains that a higher-priced product is generally considered to be a higher-quality product.

Unless you are a large retailer, such as Walmart, pricing is more of an art than it is a science. What you're trying to determine is the best price point for your company to maximize total revenue. Understanding that the price and demand curves work against each other is a critical concept in understanding the best way to price your goods or services. All other things being equal, increasing prices generally tends to lower the demand for those goods or services. This is not always the case, but it is generally so.

Let's say you're going to have a lawn sprinkler system installed at your home. If you call two or three installation companies, the chances are you will see a significant difference in the estimated cost of the project. One company may use pricing as its main method for getting jobs, while another company may use the quality of its work and years of experience as its unique selling proposition. In this case each company has made a decision, based upon its reading of the market, as to the best method for increasing revenue. Both methods have proven to be successful. In making these decisions, keep in mind that pricing structure alone does portray a powerful image to your potential customers.

If you are a customer, you must ask yourself whether or not you are more interested in a good price for the sprinkler system or in the quality and reputation of the company doing the installation. We all make judgments every day regarding price and perceived value.

Experience has taught me that I prefer to be on the higher end of the scale in pricing my company's products and services. This generally affords greater margins and therefore gives greater flexibility. It also sends a message to the marketplace—a message that I want sent. I simply find it much easier to be successful on the higher end of the pricing scale than on the lower end, where you are always competing solely on price. On the low end, a few dollars can be the difference between winning and losing a customer. There is not much flexibility on the low end.

I do not advocate being the highest priced product in the market. I just prefer to be on the higher end of the pricing scale. This is a decision that you must make in deciding on your pricing policy. Should you decide to be on the higher end of the pricing scale, you must remember that your products and services must support that pricing: your value proposition must be real.

Over the long run, you can't price a product of low quality on the high end of the scale. Also, you cannot price your services on the higher end of the scale and not provide excellent customer service. Here are some basic questions you will need to answer in deciding your pricing policy:

- How do you set product or service prices? (Desired margin, competition, image, etc.)
- How do these prices compare with your competitors?
- What customers will you attract on the high side of the pricing scale?
- What customers will you attract on the low side of the pricing scale?
- If you are on the high end of pricing, can you provide the level of quality and service required to support that pricing?
- Does your pricing support the company image you desire?

You should review your pricing at least annually. I advocate reviewing your pricing twice a year for strategic reasons: it is generally easier for your customers to accept two price increases of 2 percent than one price increase of 4 percent. In deciding which pricing is best for you, look at how you can maximize your gross margin. After all, it is the total gross margin dollars generated from revenue that will have the largest impact on your operating profit.

Here is a short refresher on how to calculate your selling price:

1. Decide on your desired margin percentage. (Remember the importance of margin to overall profitability.)
2. Compute your costs (material plus labor).
3. Subtract that desired margin percentage from one (1).
4. Divide the answer into your cost (material and labor).
5. The result is your sell price.

Example: Bob wants to calculate the price he should bid for a remodeling job his crew is doing. He wants a 45 percent gross margin in order to maintain his desired net profit. He has determined that he will have $2,000 in material costs, plus $3,000 in labor costs for total costs of $5,000. He then subtracts 45 percent from one (1). The answer is 55 percent. So he divides his cost ($5,000) by 55 percent to get a selling price of $9,090.

Note: Margin and mark-up are *not* the same. In the above example if Bob had marked up his costs by 45 percent his selling price would have been $7,250. So instead of clearing $4,090 in margin on the job, he would have cleared $2,250. This is only a 31 percent margin, not the 45 percent he needed.

Promotion and Image

Pricing policy is not the only influence on company image and customer acquisition. Your marketing plan will also have a profound effect on your company image. You will need to decide on the various avenues available to you to promote your company. Once you have decided on the primary message you want to send, you must decide on the best methods of disseminating that information to your customers.

We all see slick advertising from large companies every day. We see it in print and on television and hear it on the radio. Most of this goes right by us, but some of it sticks. Advertisers know that, and it is the main reason we see the same message over and over again. Most small businesses cannot afford this type of marketing campaign. The good news is that you do not need to be a large company to have a marketing campaign. Other methods are available to you.

Being involved in the community can be very helpful to your company image. You could join your Chamber of Commerce, although you must become involved for this to pay benefits. Join a civic organization like the Rotary club or the Lions club. Champion a cause or actively support your favorite charity.

You should also join trade organizations within your industry. Consider attending industry trade shows where you can showcase your products or services and meet potential customers.

All of these methods are in addition to any direct advertising you do to promote your company. Remember that you should never devote all of your marketing time and efforts to only one strategy. I have seen many small business owners do that, and it is a strategy for failure. Here are some questions you must answer to maximize your marketing campaign:

- What media will you use to reach your targeted audience?
- What other methods can you use to reach your audience? (Trade shows, e-mail, promotions, etc.)
- What is your primary message to customers and potential customers?

- What image do you want customers and potential customers to have of your business?
- What is your promotional and advertising budget, and how was it determined?
- What methods do you use to monitor and evaluate your marketing program?

A promotional campaign is critical to getting your message to your marketplace. Although it is not a difficult undertaking, it is an important one. Spend some time discussing the options with your team. A variety of input can be very valuable in making the right decisions. A promotional campaign should never be devised by one person; there is too much bias in that approach.

Opportunities

Once you have completed your analysis of your company, your competition, your pricing strategy, and your promotional campaign, you are in position to look at your opportunities for new revenue. That revenue may be found in a completely new area for you, maybe by adding a new product line or by providing additional services. Maybe you have discovered a potential untapped customer base. Whatever information your analysis generates about potential new customers, do not ignore the untapped potential in your current customers.

Current customers do not cost you anything in acquisition costs. They already know your company and what to expect from you. So, focus on existing customers first. How can you expand your business with them? Do they have needs beyond what you are currently providing, and which you could satisfy? We all want new customers. Just make sure you are continually maximizing your revenue potential with the customers you currently have. That is real, untapped, and inexpensive potential new revenue.

Opportunities are a vital part of any marketing campaign. They help provide for a solid future as well as potential to increase current performance. Here are a few important questions to answer when looking at opportunities:

- What are your major opportunities, based on the answers given above, to increase your business with your existing customers?
- What are your major opportunities, based on the answers given above, to increase your business with your new customers?
- What are your major opportunities to enter completely new markets?
- What do these opportunities tell you about your company image and positioning?

Threats

Threats to a company can come from both outside and inside the company. Competition and changing legal environments are classic examples of external threats. Inadequate personnel or outdated infrastructure are examples of internal threats. You must be honest in assessing and understanding the threats you face.

All businesses face competition. It is important to understand your competition's strengths and weaknesses so you can effectively compete in the marketplace. If you are losing market share to your competition, ask what other businesses are doing more successfully than you. Do they have product or service advantages? Do they provide better customer service? If they have a pricing advantage, how are you positioning your company to overcome that advantage?

Having the right personnel is critical to success, as is keeping your technology updated. We have all been exposed to companies who seem to have the wrong people working there. Maybe it was a rude waiter. Maybe it was a customer-service representative who wouldn't stop talking long enough for you to fully explain your problem. There are unlimited examples of how personnel either help or hinder a company.

You must be hard on yourself in making sure you have the right people and that they are properly placed within your company. Good people can really help you. Bad ones can kill you. Look carefully at your personnel and be willing to make any necessary tough decisions.

It is most important that you have executable plans to deal with threats. Quite often, by paying close attention to the threats against your company, you can turn a threat into an opportunity. How do you do that? Let's say you have an external competitive threat: one of your competitors is taking market share from you. By understanding how the competitor does that, you can devise a plan to take back that lost market share and turn the threat into an opportunity to reclaim revenue you are losing to your competitor. Understanding how your competition is cutting into your market share turns a threat into a potential opportunity.

Maybe you have an internal threat that is related to personnel. Perhaps your company is lacking in highly trained customer-service employees. How much additional revenue could you realize by improving your customer service? Another way to ask this is, how much business have you already lost simply due to poor customer service? Again, by analyzing the threat and devising a plan to counter the threat, you can realize an opportunity.

Here are some basic questions to ask yourself regarding threats:

- What internal threats (personnel, technology, etc.) may prevent you from reaching your goals?
- What external threats (competition, environmental, legal, etc.) may prevent you from reaching your goals?
- What contingency plans do you have to deal with external threats?
- How can you create opportunity from those threats?

Here is a form you can use to do this analysis. It requires that you think carefully about strengths, weaknesses, opportunities, and threats. This form is generic, so it can be used to analyze your company as well as your competition. Not all items on the form will be applicable to all situations. Change the categories as needed for your situation.

Basic SWOT Analysis

	Strength	Weakness	Opportunity	Threat
Market Share				
Ability to compete with closest competitor				
Ease of entry into market				
Changing technology as it affects current products or services				
Competitive pricing				
Distribution channels				
Geographic location				
Availability of needed workforce skillset				
Managerial experience				
Financial strength				
Manufacturing capabilities				
Workforce experience				
Customer service commitment				

Responsiveness of workforce				
Physical infrastructure				
Use of technology				
Regulatory environment				

Basic Marketing Categories

Below, I've listed some of the most common marketing categories to consider. For each category I've included a basic definition, what skills are required to utilize it, and basic cost information. Use this as a guide in deciding which marketing strategies work best for your company. I would never advocate putting all of your eggs in one basket. You should use multiple marketing categories in order to reach the broadest number of potential customers. Be sure to track the success of each strategy to refine your marketing program.

Here they are.

1. **Networking**

    a. Basics:

    Get out there and start meeting with other people to talk about your product or service. Networking can include going to trade shows, speaking at seminars, participating in discussion boards, and going to local chamber of commerce meetings or other places where business people gather. Networking is a form of business oriented socializing.

    b. Skills:

    You need to believe in yourself and whatever product or service you provide. You must also be able to talk about your product. Industry knowledge is very helpful. If you are naturally gregarious, this will be easy for you, if not, just focus on the specific knowledge you have to offer.

c. Time and Money:
Networking takes time. Attending trade shows can be very expensive. You must force yourself to do as much of this type of marketing as you can afford, both in time and money. It always pays off. Networking is a long-term strategy.

2. **Direct-Mail Marketing**
a. Basics:
Direct mail marketing includes sales letters, brochures, and flyers. We all get these every day. With the rise of e-mail marketing, direct mail has fallen off. But in the right situation, it can still be used effectively. Just make sure you understand that only about 2 percent of your target audience will respond to a direct mail offering—and that is considered a good response rate.

b. Skills:
You will need writing skills. If you don't have these skills, you might consider hiring a professional. Additionally, you will need a list of business prospects and their addresses.

c. Time and Money:
You will incur expenses for printing and mailing, as well as possibly fees for a graphic artist and a writer. It is a short-term strategy that is designed to bring you immediate leads or sales.

3. **Media Advertising**
a. Basics:
TV, radio, magazine and newspaper ads are all traditional forms of advertising that are used to raise brand awareness. Most

industries have a variety of trade journals that are a good choice for long-term advertising to potential customers.

b. Skills:
Generally, the outlet in which you choose to advertise will have people to help you create a good ad campaign.

c. Time and Money
This can be expensive. It is generally a long-term strategy that is used to build brand awareness over an extended period of time.

4. **Offline Advertising**
   a. Basics:
   This includes classified advertising, business cards, flyers, and promotional items with your business name on them—buttons, hats, and pencils.

   b. Skills:
   You will need the ability to write short ads.

   c. Time and Money:
   It is less expensive than traditional advertising, but it has less reach. Classified advertising is a short-term strategy that should bring immediate benefits.

5. **Training Programs**
   a. Basics:
   A training program might be set up in several ways:
   Online training—you set up a course online.
   Training at your customer's place of business: you would travel to a company and teach your course.

Training at your own place of business: you would set up the meeting place and find people to attend. You might develop a training program to increase awareness of your products.

b. Skills:
You'll need to be able to write a syllabus and course materials as well as teach the course.

c. Time and Money:
This could be time intensive. You will have to set up the course and find the time to teach it. You may have to rent a place to teach.

6. **Become Known as an Expert**
   a. Basics:
   In order to become recognized as an expert, you will need to give out advice that gets immediate results. Generally, you will start out by giving free advice. When you get a little notoriety, you can start publishing and charging for your advice.

   b. Skills:
   In order to become an expert, you are going to need skills in at least one of the following areas: writing, creating plans, or public speaking.

   c. Time and Money:
   This is a time intensive strategy, but it can pay big dividends. We have all come across people who are billed as experts. These "experts" have one thing in common: they all put in a great deal of time learning their subject long before they became known

as an expert. Publishing is very time consuming and requires an up-front time commitment. Consider electronic publishing as your initial strategy.

7. **Press Releases**

   a. Basics:

   Local newspapers are always looking for content to fill their pages. Sending them press releases can be a good way to increase awareness of your company, especially if you are a new entry into the market.

   b. Skills:

   You will need to learn how to write and distribute your press releases. You may need to hire a professional publicist, but the newspaper will edit the copy you send.

   c. Time and Money:

   This is considered a risky tactic. There are no guarantees that any newspaper will print your press release. If you do the writing yourself, it is not expensive. However, if you hire an agency, it can be very expensive.

8. **Website**

   a. Basics:

   Today every business has a website, and one is often expected by your potential customers as a form of validation. You are certainly at a disadvantage without a website.

   b. Skills:

   You will either need to learn how to build a site yourself, or you can hire a professional. Websites can be simple or complicated and everything in between. If you are planning on doing e-commerce, then I highly recommend that you hire a professional website developer.

c. Time and Money:
Currently websites range from $3,000 to $5,000 for a simple website all the way up to hundreds of thousands of dollars for complicated websites.

9. **Internet Advertising**
a. Basics:
This involves advertising on search engines or popular social websites. We all see these banners and pop-ups every day as we browse the web. If Internet traffic is critical to your business, then you should consult with a search engine optimizer (SEO).

b. Skills:
It seems unrealistic to think of doing this on your own unless you are a search engine optimizer yourself. This field is now so specialized it only seems logical to consult with an expert.

c. Time and Money:
Internet ads are relatively inexpensive since you usually pay per click—that is, you only pay for people who actually visit your website. That is a pretty good methodology. You should count on it taking up to six months for you to see any real results.

Marketing Goals

Now that you have done a SWOT analysis and understand the basic marketing methodologies, it is time to set some goals and then formulate a marketing plan that will allow you to achieve those goals. Here are some questions you will need to answer:

- What are your twelve-month goals? (Sales forecast)
- What are your three- to five-year goals? (Long-term projections)
- How will you measure your success toward achieving these goals?

Once you have answered these questions, you have written a basic marketing plan. You may want to flesh it out more, but the basics will be there. Below is a general marketing plan I have used for many years that can be modified to meet your needs. You must write down answers to all of the questions. This becomes your executable plan for the next year and beyond. It is important to completely revise your marketing plan every year. One of the biggest mistakes you can make is to write a plan and not revisit it at least annually.

Strategic Marketing Plan

Company Name_____
Date_____

Market Analysis

Describe your customers._____
_____
_____
_____
_____
_____

What are your customers' needs?_____
_____
_____
_____
_____
_____

Who is your target market? (Can be type of customer or specific targets)

Current market	New targets
_____	_____
_____	_____
_____	_____
_____	_____
_____	_____
_____	_____

Products or services and their benefits

Product	Benefits
_____	_____
_____	_____
_____	_____
_____	_____
_____	_____
_____	_____
_____	_____

Unique Selling Proposition (USP) Why should someone do business with you?

Your USP must be supportable and instantly recognizable within your company. It should not include the word "quality." Whether or not it is true, all businesses claim to deliver quality, so a selling proposition that cites "quality" cannot be unique.

_____
_____
_____
_____
_____
_____

Your SWOT Analysis

Strengths_____
_____
_____
_____

Weaknesses_____
_____
_____
_____

Opportunities_____
_____
_____
_____

Threats_____
_____
_____
_____

Competitive Analysis

Competitor's Name_____
Strengths_____

Weaknesses_____

Competitor's advantage_____

Competitor's Name_____
Strengths_____

Weaknesses_____

Competitor's advantage_____

Competitor's Name_____
Strengths_____

Weaknesses_____

Competitor's advantage_____

Goals

	Annual		Quarterly

Year Ending_____Qtr. Ending_____
Revenue_____Revenue_____
Gross Margin %_____Gross Margin %_____
Operating Profit $_____Op. Profit $_____
Cash on hand_____Cash on hand_____

(Note: these are examples of possible goals. You must insert the goals important to your company)

Key strategies to achieving the goals (e.g., open new markets, improve customer service, improve efficiency, add new products or services)

1._____

2._____

3._____

4._____

5._____
_____

(Note: prioritize your strategies by immediate impact on your goals)

Tactics and Accountability (Specific actions you will undertake to support your key strategies)

Tactic	When it will be executed	Who is responsible
_____	_____	_____
_____	_____	_____
_____	_____	_____
_____	_____	_____
_____	_____	_____
_____	_____	_____
_____	_____	_____
_____	_____	_____
_____	_____	_____

Critical numbers (The two or three numbers that tell you, at a glance, if your strategies are working—sales growth over prior period, number of new customers, increased production efficiency, etc.)

1._____
2._____
3._____

Marketing Activities

(Attend trade show, advertise in periodicals, direct mail, promotions, etc.)

Activity	Cost

Have a Customer-Centric Focus

The moment you realize that all the analysis and planning you do will only take you as far as your commitment to your customers is an epiphany. Planning is critical; there is no doubt about that. However, to succeed in business you can't just be "as good" as the next guy. You must be demonstrably better and be able to prove it. Here we will discuss ways that you can explode your business.

Some time ago I had an experience that made me realize why so many businesses fail. I went to a neighborhood store and arrived there five minutes before opening. I walked through the unlocked front door about fifteen feet into the store and heard someone yell, "We don't open for five minutes!" I looked around the store and saw two groups of employees standing and chatting with each other. None were busy with work.

When the woman told me the store was not open yet, meaning I needed to exit the store and wait five minutes while the employees finished chatting, I thought she was joking. She wasn't! She had seen me walking in the door and deliberately stopped me from doing business that day. How absurd! Here I went out of my way to buy something, and I was not allowed the "privilege" of giving the store my money.

Sadly, this is all too common in business today—a totally apathetic attitude toward the customer. It appeared to me that the person who accosted me that morning had absolutely no respect for customers. Now think about it: how many people do you do business with repeatedly who have no respect for you? I wouldn't think too many. So why do people think that they can treat others with apathy and still keep their customers?

By the way, this person was not the owner of the store. She was an employee. Some may feel that it's not the fault of the business owner that she treated me like this. But it is! Obviously, the owner has not made it clear that customer service is the employee's number one priority. I can't imagine any of Disney World's employees treating their "guests" like that.

Let's look at what I might be worth to that store. Let's assume that I spend $20 a week there, and I'll be a customer for the next five years. That means that they'll have $5,200 less business in those five years. Now, let's say the employee who accosted me had worked there for only two months, but she caused four other people like me to stop doing business there. That's $26,000 in lost business—a very costly mistake.

Now think of those businesses or people with whom you would continue to do business even if it became inconvenient for you. Why do you continue to patronize them? Maybe it is because the business makes you feel special and they appreciate you. I can think of a hair stylist who has clients that drive sixty miles to see him; he's booked three months in advance, and he charges more than most hair stylists. How he can do that? The answer is simple: by concentrating on customers first, giving them what they want, and treating them as if they were special.

If you're thinking that this is obvious stuff and wondering what it has to do with using targeted marketing techniques, here is the answer: You can use all of those marketing techniques perfectly, but if you don't have good customer service, you won't succeed in the long term. Good customer service is the foundation of any solid business. This may be common sense, but many businesses ignore it. You do so at your own peril.

Here is a scenario for you to think about. Bob is a new arrival in your town or city and is interested in your service. Through casual conversation you realize that Bob is in the market for your services. Here are some questions for you:

- Why should Bob do business with you?
- What makes you better than your nearest competitor?

I don't want to hear anything about how good the quality of your service is, that you're number one, or anything about how long the company has been around. It all makes a good story but won't get you long-term customers. Here's the final question: Can you tell me in thirty seconds why I should do business with you?

You would be amazed at the number of business people who can't provide a satisfactory answer to this simple question. Or, even worse, their answer is indistinguishable from that of their competitors.

Remember, when it is all said and done, there are only three ways to increase revenue. First, you can increase the size of each transaction with current customers. Second, you can increase the number of transactions with current customers. Third, you can get new customers. It may seem simple, but that's it. There is nothing else.

In fashioning a marketing plan, it is important to realize that two of the three ways to increase your revenue are with current customers. Avoid the temptation to only focus on getting new customers while neglecting the "care and feeding" of your current customer base.

There are several ways to increase the size of the transaction with your current customer. You are basically trying to add value to the transaction while creating or maintaining a bond with your customer, which is essentially a bond of trust. You would not want to violate that trust by trying to increase the size of the transaction solely for your own benefit. The customer must understand that the recommendation you are making is for his benefit. So look for ways to increase the size of the transaction without decreasing the trust you have with your customer.

Since the cost of obtaining a new customer is significantly greater than the cost of maintaining a current customer, it is also important to increase the number of transactions you have with each of your current customers. The easiest way to get customers to return to you frequently is to treat them well. You can also develop specific programs or strategies, such as monthly specials, product updates, or add-ons to get them to return more frequently.

Finally, the third way to increase revenue is to increase the number of customers you have. This is the main focus of most marketing programs. However this is only one of three ways to increase revenue. You must protect against making this your only focus, as it will detract from the focus on current customers.

This is not to say that there is not a need for a marketing program to continually address the acquisition of new customers. The basic methods for getting new customers involve targeted leads, referrals, advertising, networking, trade shows, and so on. However, by combining a detailed marketing program with a focused customer retention program you can maximize your opportunity to grow the company and continually increase revenue.

It really comes down to your company orientation. Is your focus on customers, or is it on internal operations? Currently the news is full of a plethora of General Motors recalls. There seems to be almost one every month. These constant recalls are a direct result of General Motors' internal focus. There is clearly a corporate willingness to put the needs of the company (internal focus) ahead of the needs of the customers.

The new CEO of General Motors, Mary Barra, has inherited an abundance of problems from the previous management team. Her biggest challenge is not to make it through the recalls, as some people think. It is to change the culture of the company so all employees think about what is best for their customers before they think about what is best for General Motors. If the employees put the interests of their customers first and foremost in their thoughts, General Motors can emerge as a stronger company. We will see if that happens.

To bring all this into perspective, here is a good table (not my creation) that will help you identify what kind of business you have. You must be honest in your analysis of your business. Wishful thinking gets you nowhere here. So look carefully at this chart, and identify whether your company is customer or production oriented. If you make billions of widgets all day long, then you can afford to be production oriented. If not, you need to be customer oriented.

Topic	Customer Orientation	Production Orientation
Attitude toward customers.	Customers' needs determine company plans	They should be glad we exist to help them!
Product offering	The company makes or offers what its customers want	Better products at less cost
Innovation	Use innovation to locate new opportunities and assist customers	Focus on technology as a means of cost cutting
Profitability	The critical objective	The residual. What is left after all costs are covered
Role of customer credit	Seen as an integral part of good customer service	Seen as a necessary evil
Role of packaging	Designed with the customer in mind and as a selling tool	Seen as merely a protection for the product
Inventory levels	Set with customer needs and costs in mind	Set with production needs in mind
Advertising	Stresses satisfaction of needs and addresses customer wants	Stresses product quality
Sales force	To help customers find the product that best fits their needs	Sell the customer what we make!

Product Introductions

We have talked about the three ways to increase revenue. Introducing new products or services can help you increase revenue in all three ways. New products can bring in new customers, increase the number of transactions with current customers, and sometimes increase the size of each transaction with your current customers. However, one very important aspect of product introductions is often overlooked—the failure to recognize that your first customers are always internal.

It is critical to understand that before you can expect your sales force or your customer-service department to fully get behind a new product, you must first sell them on the product. If you think you can just expect them to fully support a new product simply because they are employees, you are sadly mistaken. You have to sell the product to your employees before you can expect them to sell it to the external customers of the company.

How do you do that? By getting employees involved in the process as early as possible. It is always a mistake to wait until a product is about to be launched to introduce it to your internal customers (e.g., sales force, customer service). You want them fully on board. You want them to believe in the benefits and differentiating factors of the product. After all, if they don't fully support the product, how can you expect them to sell that product to their customers? It just doesn't make sense. Yet it happens every day.

I recently purchased new carpet for my home. During the process we developed a good relationship with a particular sales person at a local flooring company. As we were going through the selection process we asked him about a carpet that had just recently been introduced to the market. Even though the product was from a very reputable company, the sales person directed us away from it. His reasoning was that he was not sure the carpet would do everything the manufacturer said it would. This is a classic case of the company ignoring their first customers. So we bought a different carpet that the sales person had complete faith in.

Unfortunately, I have seen this scenario over and over again. A company has an idea for a great new product. Management has completed the design stage, the development, the testing, and the marketing plan, all while ignoring their sales force. So when the great product is finally introduced, management suddenly realizes they must get their sales force on board if they want to sell any of the product. So management has a one-day "product training" session and is somehow stunned when their own sales force is skeptical.

So, get your internal customers involved early. Keep them in the loop and inside the tent. Let them have input. Their input will probably turn out to be valuable, and you have won them over already just by getting them involved. Your product introductions will be much more successful if you follow this path than if you wait until the last minute to get internal customers on board. In doing this, remember that your internal customers are not just your sales force; they are also your customer-service personnel. Without their support, it will be difficult to successfully introduce new products.

Effective Methods for Managing People

Finding, keeping, and managing good personnel are major challenges facing any small business. Think of managing people as a never-ending challenge. It is not a project; it is an ongoing process. Motivating employees to consistently deliver quality is critical to business success, particularly for a service business. Yet motivating people is a very misunderstood concept. My experience is that you cannot motivate a fundamentally unmotivated person. The most you can hope to do is to influence that person.

Owners must communicate the company's goals effectively and then train their employees to help achieve those goals. This never-ending process requires not only perseverance but also understanding. Generally, managers rely on training to ensure that their staff is competent and has the right attitude. However, all the training in the world will not overcome hiring the wrong people and an employee's lack of effective communication skills. Hire well, and you will live well.

Compensation

Compensation (e.g., salary, bonuses) can be used to help motivate employees to adopt an attitude of adding value to the company. However, compensation alone will not accomplish this task. Recognition of exceptional performance is just as important as compensation. People like to be recognized for going above and beyond. It makes them feel appreciated, and that feeling of appreciation is one of the most powerful means you have of giving your employees a sense that they bring real value to the company.

Since most small businesses cannot compete with corporate America in compensation, a willingness to show appreciation for good work becomes even more important in staff retention. The small business owner has a fundamental decision to make: How to stay competitive in the labor market without breaking the bank. Sometimes it comes down to deciding what is more important to the company, short-term savings on compensation or long-term added value. I vote for long-term value. Ultimately, that is all that matters.

Benefits

Benefits (e.g., health insurance, paid time off, retirement plans) are very difficult to manage. You will need to offer some benefits if you want to attract good people, but they have become very expensive. Here also, small businesses generally cannot compete with the benefits offered by large corporations. That is a fact that must be faced and dealt with. It is wonderful to be able to offer benefits, but you must be careful to not get locked in to a situation where your desire to offer benefits has a significant negative effect on profitability.

Remember that unless your profitability is sufficient to allow you to reinvest in your company, all the benefits packages in the world are meaningless. In that situation, your employees will have to share a larger portion of the cost of benefits. Do not hide this from them. Rather, share it. Employees need to know that you are being open and honest with them. I have yet to see a case where being honest with employees did not yield the most desirable long-term outcome for the business.

Interviewing the Candidate

Prior to the interview, determine the skills, knowledge, and experience needed to perform the job to be filled. Make sure to get adequate input from people, whose opinion you trust, before making these determinations. Try to refine your requirements into areas that can be measured in some way. What range of experience, level of knowledge is needed? Do you have a test of any kind that would assist in determining that level of knowledge? Do not go into any interview without having asked and answered these fundamental questions.

I never hire from just one interview. I have found that you simply cannot get enough information from one interview to allow you to make a good hiring decision. Also, make sure more than one person conducts the interview. Multiple opinions can point to the red flags that tell you which candidates to avoid. Rarely will you come across a candidate that you are positive is the best person for the job. You are more likely to make a "best guess" judgment call. The more information and opinions you have to inform that judgment, the better the chances you have of making a good hiring decision.

My experience is that the most effective interviews are conversational in nature. While it is important to have a set of questions to ask, it is also important to make the interview a conversation, not an interrogation. Use as many open-ended questions as you can. Avoid asking too many questions that have a one-word answer. Your questions should be designed to get the candidate to tell you about himself. You not only need to know whether or not the candidate is capable, experienced, and qualified; you also need to know if the candidate is a good fit for your company. Here are some open-ended questions you might use:

- Which of your previous jobs did you like the most? Why?
- Which of your former jobs did you like the least? Why?
- What is your ideal job and why?
- Tell me about a time when your actions made a positive difference in a difficult situation.
- What was the most difficult challenge you overcame in your previous positions?

Once you have asked a question, resist the urge to expound. Just listen to the response. Try not to interrupt the candidate's train of thought. You want the candidate to talk to you in his own style. This gives you insight into the candidate's thought processes. Listen, listen, and listen. Also, while it is expected that you will take notes, don't look like you're writing a book. That only makes people nervous.

Interviews are always a two-way street. While you are interviewing the candidate, keep in mind that the candidate is also interviewing you. Do you fit with the wants of the candidate? He is making the same assessment about you that you are making about him. Give a brief history of your company. What industry are you in? Who are your customers? Who are your competitors? Even if the candidate is not the best fit for your company, you should still try to sell the candidate on what you have to offer. Candidates want to know that there is a future with your company. People talk to each other, and your reputation as a good place to work is an important business asset.

Often you will be faced with a virtual tie between candidates following the interviews. As a matter of fact, this is generally more often the case than it is not. That is when it is even more important than ever to consider each candidate's long-term potential. Who can help your company the most over the long haul? I know it is popular today to say there is no such thing as a candidate being overqualified. I think that is dangerous thinking. I wouldn't reject a candidate solely because he or she seems overqualified, but I do know from experience that it is a factor worth considering. That is when you have a frank conversation with the candidate. Tell him or her your concerns and then listen carefully to the response. He or she may very well have a good reason why you need not be concerned about this issue. Give him or her the opportunity to tell you so. You may pick up a gem if you give the candidate the chance to show you how valuable he or she can be to you.

The interview process must comply with the law, which is extensive and complicated. Do not try to be an expert here; that is a recipe for disaster. Check with legal counsel or with human resource experts to make sure you are compliant. One misstep here can be of great consequence to you and to your company.

Maintaining Good Employee Relations

There is probably nothing more important to the long-term success of any company than having a good relationship with its employees. <u>No organization can be any more successful than the collective ability and commitment of its employees to that mutual success.</u> If your employees think it is acceptable to do mediocre work, then that is exactly what you will get. This always decreases the value of any company. It is a very straight one-to-one correlation. So how do you get top performance out of employees? The answer is easy: hire well and maintain a good relationship with your employees. However, just because the answer is easy does not mean the implementation will also be easy. It rarely is.

Trust is central to beneficial employee relationships. Employees are people. People want to know they can trust the people around them. That goes for fellow employees as well as for management. If your employees do not feel they can trust the information you provide, they will not be fully committed to the company. To think otherwise is to fundamentally misunderstand your employees. Obviously, you cannot share every piece of information, but when you can share, you should. This helps keep everyone on the same page and builds trust. It also helps to break down any walls that may have formed between employees and management.

Training is also important to the relationship of trust. Be willing to give employees as much training as they want as long as that training is important to the future of the company. Training is not free, but done correctly it pays big dividends. Training allows you to promote from within. There is not much more you can do to motivate an ambitious employee than showing her that the company is willing to invest in her future. As others see this upward mobility, they see opportunity for themselves. This is critical to getting more employees committed to their own success and the success of the company.

Performance Reviews

Employees deserve to know how well they are doing in their job. One of the mechanisms for doing this is a performance review. It is less common for hourly workers to have a formal performance review than for salaried employees. Generally, if you are having problems with an hourly worker, chances are that you or the supervisor has discussed the issue with the employee at the time the issue arose. Also, any employees working under a collective bargaining agreement are probably covered by a progressive discipline section of that agreement.

Regular review of salaried employee performance is very important. It lets the employees know what they are doing well and where they need to improve. This review is also usually the mechanism for any increases in compensation. You will have established ranges of compensation for each position tied to performance. In order for your employees to progress through the range, they need to know the areas where they can improve.

Performance reviews have become more and more complex in recent years. I find this complexity to be utterly unnecessary and fundamentally without value. My preference is simply to use a review structure that addresses the eight to ten general areas of performance (more if the employee is a supervisor) and then to assign numeric values to the achieved performance in each area. The sum of all the assigned values is then divided by the total number of areas being evaluated to arrive at a final number. The final number is used to make any decisions regarding pay increases and bonuses. I like to use a five-point evaluation system, but that is personal preference. Below is an example of a performance review (not of my creation) that is applicable to most situations. Personalize it to meet your needs.

The performance levels are defined in the beginning of the review. There is no need to fixate on deciding which numeric value to assign to a specific area. Consistency is much more important here. Evaluate each area on the same scale and with the same level of consistency. Also, use the same evaluation methodology for all employees being evaluated.

Employee Performance Appraisal

*Employee Name*_____
*Manager Name*_____
*Job Title*_____
*Prepared By*_____
*Hire Date*_____
*Review Date*_____

Ratings

Outstanding (5): Exceptional performance in all areas of responsibility. Planned objectives were achieved well above the established standards with significant accomplishments made.

Exceeds Expectations (4): Consistently exceeds established standards in most areas of responsibility. All requirements were met, and objectives were achieved above the established standards.

Meets Expectations (3): All job requirements were met, and planned objectives were accomplished within established standards.

Needs Improvement (2): Performance in one or more critical areas does not meet expectations. Not all planned objectives were accomplished.

Does Not Meet Minimum Standards (1): Does not meet minimum job requirements. Performance is unacceptable. Responsibilities are not being met, and important objectives have not been accomplished. Needs immediate improvement.

<u>Factors to Evaluate</u>

Please assign a rating (from list on first page) and give examples for each of the following factors:

Knowledge
Specific to Profession—Technical concepts
Rating: _____

_____
_____
_____
_____

Specific to Company—Methods, Procedures and Policies
Rating: _____

_____
_____
_____
_____

Quality
Overall accuracy, completeness of assignments and attention to detail
Rating: _____

_____
_____
_____
_____

Quantity
Efficient use of time; ability to meet deadlines and overall productivity
Rating: _____

_____
_____
_____
_____

Communication Skills
Information conveyed in a clear and concise manner, both written and verbal
Rating: _____

_____
_____
_____
_____

Interpersonal Skills
Ability to interact and work with clients, coworkers, and manager
Rating: _____

_____
_____
_____
_____

Adaptability
Effectively adjusts to changes in routines, processes, and deadlines
Rating: _____

_____
_____
_____
_____

Initiative
Takes action to complete what is necessary in the absence of specific direction
Rating: _____

_____
_____
_____
_____

Judgment
Takes appropriate action under given circumstances
Rating: _____

_____
_____
_____
_____

Safety Practices
Performs work in a safe manner
Rating: _____

_____
_____
_____
_____

Problem Solving
Ingenuity or resourcefulness; finding new or better technology or methodology to accomplish goals, reduce costs, save time, or improve quality
Rating: _____

_____
_____
_____
_____

Attendance
Rating: _____

_____
_____
_____
_____

<u>Supervisory Factors to Evaluate</u>

For employees with supervisory responsibilities, please assign a rating (from list on first page) and give examples for each of the following factors:

Supervision of Others
Clarity of instructions and guidance given to subordinates
Rating: _____

_____
_____
_____
_____

MICHAEL D LACEY

Leadership
Inspires teamwork
Rating: _____

_____
_____
_____
_____

Organization
Efficient in planning, scheduling, delegating, and utilizing staff
Rating: _____

_____
_____
_____
_____

Drive for Results
Department goals and deadlines met timely and efficiently
Rating: _____

_____
_____
_____
_____

Training and Development
Trains direct reports and assists employees in development of new skills
Rating: _____

_____
_____
_____
_____

Compliance with Company Policy
Meets objectives within established guidelines
Rating: _____

_____
_____
_____
_____

Fiscal Responsibility
Plans and adheres to department budget
Rating: _____

_____
_____
_____
_____

<u>Strengths and Professional Development</u>

Strengths
_____
_____
_____
_____

Areas for professional development or additional training
_____
_____
_____
_____

Development Plan

_____
_____
_____
_____
_____

Employee Overall Performance Number (1 to 5) Rating: _____
(Total of individual areas rated divided by number of areas rated)

Employee Comments

_____
_____
_____
_____
_____

The employee's supervisor signs below to indicate understanding of the content of the appraisal. The employee then signs to confirm that he or she has reviewed the content of the evaluation with his or her supervisor. The employee's signature does not indicate agreement or disagreement with everything stated on this evaluation. Please attach a separate page for additional employee comments.

Signatures

Employee _____ Date _____

Supervisor _____ Date _____

By evaluating employees in this way, you will identify your top performers as well as those who consistently underperform. You will want to reward your top performers and decide how to deal with the underperformers. I feel strongly that any employee who does not achieve a rating of at least a three needs immediate attention. An employee with an overall rating of less than three is holding you back and merits a serious discussion. A rating less than three does not mean you terminate that employee. It may mean that she needs more training or has been poorly assigned in her current position. Use your judgment, but do not avoid the issue.

One note of caution: interpret evaluations with regard to the expected future of the employee. If you have targeted an employee for future management, then your scale slides upward somewhat. I can't imagine targeting an employee who does not consistently have superior evaluations as a future leader. Be honest in your evaluations and forward thinking in what you do with the results.

Bonuses and Compensation Increases

Bonuses are now expected by almost all employees; they often factor a bonus into their personal spending habits. I have seen many instances where a bonus not yet received has already been spent. (There was a good parody of this in the movie *Christmas Vacation*.)

The first decision point for any bonus should be company performance. If the company has not met its overall performance objectives, there should not be any bonuses, period. It is critical that you convey this requirement immediately upon instituting any company bonus program. Failure to make sure that all employees understand that company performance is the starting point for any possible bonuses will result in unhappy employees and long-term resentment.

If the company does meet the target performance, then, and only then, would you move on to assigning individuals a bonus. A two-tiered approach to bonuses has always worked for me, offering senior management the opportunity to earn a bonus of a certain percentage of their annual salary. I have used a range of 10 to 20 percent, providing the company can afford that.

With first- and midlevel managers, I simply assign bonus amounts. This is at a lower rate than the bonus opportunity for senior management but still high enough to be of value to the employee. The exact number will depend on company performance, cash flow, capital investment needs, and so forth. Just make sure this information is relayed so there will be no misunderstanding.

For senior management the bonus requires computation. Let's say the company made the targeted budget numbers, and therefore bonuses are applicable. An employee qualifying for a 20 percent bonus would have that number impacted by one or two other factors. The first is the employee's performance evaluation. Let's say the employee had a final overall rating of 4.0 on a scale of 1 to 5. That is 80 percent of the total possible score, so his or her bonus is also 80 percent of the total possible reward. Then there is the factor of the department's performance—if this employee is in charge of a department. Let's say that number was also 80 percent of potential target. Therefore, the employee's final bonus number would be multiplied by 80 percent twice. In this example, an employee qualifying for a $10,000 bonus would receive a bonus of $6,400 ($10,000 x 80% x 80%).

In my experience this works well because employees can understand it and doesn't feel that you are just throwing darts at a dartboard to establish a bonus amount. You are actually calculating the bonus based on performance. It gives your top performing employees a true reason to excel. They know they can impact their income.

Much the same methodology is used in determining increases in compensation. First, look at what the company can afford. Then look at current compensation level increases based in continued performance. Finally, look at performance evaluations in determining any increases in compensation. This is not a straightforward calculation. It is a much more a subjective look at what you are currently paying, how the company is performing, what is reasonable in the market, and finally, employee performance. Any discussion of increases in compensation is best had at the time of the performance evaluation. That is not to say you need to decide on a final number then; you probably can't at that point. But the employees should know how all of these factors would affect their compensation.

This system uses bonuses to reward past performance and compensation to incentivize continued performance. Taken together, this evaluation and compensation system can work well for both the employee and the company. After all, one cannot prosper without the other. Both the company and the company's employees are inextricably tied to each other. It is not the only system you can use, but it works because it does tie the futures of the company and the employees to each other. That is exactly what you want.

Handling Employee Discipline

Proper disciplining of employees is difficult at best. I can't say that I have ever found a perfect system to follow. I do believe there is a distinction to be made between directed discipline and imposed punishment. To me, punishment tends to be an emotional reaction to a situation, while discipline is directed toward changing unacceptable behavior. The ultimate punishment an employer can impose on an employee is termination. Taking that approach means that anything short of termination should be targeted at behavior modification. My parents imposed a system of discipline that, if I followed it, guided me away from an undesirable consequence.

There is a great deal of literature on effective methods of discipline, and I am certainly not an authority on the subject. However, I have found that the more complicated the process becomes, the more confusing and less manageable it gets. Discipline can be as simple as telling someone who is making personal phone calls that such behavior is unacceptable. With a good employee, that may be all you need to do. If that works, then the discipline ends with its purpose accomplished.

Probably the most common problem is an employee who is too often late to work. Surprisingly enough, I have had employees who thought that the time they were supposed to report for work was a guideline, not a requirement. (A salesperson of mine in Washington, DC once said those exact words to me.) Strange, but true. Most often a simple conversation with the employee will correct the problem without any further disciplining needed. However, that is not always the case.

Human resource experts broadly recommend a system of progressive discipline for more difficult situations. Progressive discipline means that an unacceptable behavior is dealt with in ever-stronger terms the longer the behavior continues. The first offense may simply result in a warning, while continued offenses may result in termination. You can expect this to be a part of any agreement for your employees who are covered under collective bargaining.

I think the important issues to be addressed in any progressive discipline system are clarity, brevity, and recognition that some issues are more impactful than others. Clarity is important so everyone knows what constitutes a breach and what to expect from it. You can't list every possible breach, but you should take the time to list the obvious ones. Brevity, being straight and to the point, is important in keeping the system from becoming overly complicated and therefore confusing. If it takes a lawyer to interpret the system, you are in trouble. If all breaches are treated equally, you have a poor system. Why? Because it is a much bigger problem if an employee continually violates an established safety protocol than if an employee is occasionally late to work. This should be obvious. So define your system with clarity and brevity while recognizing that not all offenses are equal.

Not all infractions fall under progressive discipline. Theft and vandalism are two infractions that need no progressive discipline. Purposely injuring someone in the workplace also falls outside the requirements of progressive discipline. Make sure all employees are made aware of your discipline rules and process. You don't want a terminated employee to sue you because he or she was never made aware of the workplace rules. Just use common sense here.

Equality is also an important issue. All people may have been created equal, but it is your responsibility to make sure all employment processes are equal. Discipline should also be applied equally to all employees. If you tolerated one employee being late to work six times (and documented that) before terminating him or her for cause, you cannot then terminate another employee for tardiness after the first occurrence. Unless there are other circumstances, an attorney will more than likely become involved in such situations. I don't like this environment, but I do recognize that it exists.

Finally, don't let the system run your business. Common sense goes a long way in your approach to employees. Most people are reasonable and just want the same from you. There will be people who, no matter what you do, simply cannot be pleased. However, the majority of people just want you to be straight, honest, and fair.

The Importance of Documentation

In a litigious society, it is more important than ever to properly document employee discipline. Without proper documentation, you are completely vulnerable to legal recourse. My experience is that you cannot have too much documentation. Each employee file should reflect any and all issues you have had with that employee. It must also contain the employment application, all performance reviews, any forms signed by the employee, all warning notices, awards, and so forth. You don't need to be an expert on employment practices or human resources to know that documentation is critical in today's business environment.

Documentation is usually much more extensive in a large corporation than in a small company. Large corporations have human resource departments that document everything to the utmost degree. Small companies may have one person handling human resource issues who also has many other responsibilities. Since there is a difference in knowledge levels and capabilities between the large corporation and the small business, it can be beneficial to retain an outside human resources firm to ensure compliance with relevant laws. This is especially important regarding company policies and employee manuals.

There is no reason to spend a great amount of time and effort worrying about proper documentation when an outside human resources firm is available to help you. Retaining an outside firm is usually money well spent, especially for setting up a progressive discipline program.

Employment Law

To say that employment law has become very complicated is an understatement. No one but an attorney specializing in employment law could possibly keep up with all of the changes. There are federal laws, state laws, and court rulings, and so on to be aware of. Some states laws are friendlier to employees and others to employers. Legal counsel is best to handle all of these issues.

One issue that continually comes up is the doctrine of "Employment at Will." The simplified version of this doctrine is that both the employee and the employer have entered into an agreement regarding employment at the free will of both parties, and it can easily be terminated at the free will of either party. Notice this is a two-way street. Either party can exercise free will to terminate the relationship. That said, numerous laws govern employment at will.

When I first started my working career an employer could terminate employment for virtually any reason. It was a common joke that your boss could fire you because he didn't like the color of your shirt. As farfetched as that seems, technically it was true. Employers essentially didn't need a reason to terminate you.

Now there are laws that limit an employer's ability to terminate at will. It doesn't matter if you think these laws are good or bad. They are a fact of life. I'm not going to go into all the exceptions to employment at will, as I am not an attorney. However, here are some of the common exceptions: almost any type of discrimination, union contracts, special wartime laws, and individual employment contracts. Just make sure your employee's manual has the proper wording regarding employment at will. Check with both your attorney and a human resources specialist. This is money well spent.

Culture of Inclusion

All companies have a culture. That culture can be one of inclusion or it can be one of exclusion. I firmly believe that one of the more serious mistakes employers make is not fostering a culture of inclusion. So, what does inclusion look like? Basically, it is the willingness to share information. Not sharing information leads to distrust. You can't blame employees if they are skeptical of an employer's motives if they are never told how the company is doing. This is not radical; it is basic human nature. So share information as much as possible.

In a privately held company, it is not practical to give employees detailed financial information. But that does not mean you cannot let your employees know, in as concrete terms as feasible, about the financial health of the company where they work. Basically, any employee simply wants to know if he has a future at his current place of employment. I have never understood why so many employers see this concept as radical. Employees have mortgages to pay, kids to feed, and hopes for the future. In these critical areas, everyone wants surety above uncertainty.

If you think about it carefully, you will see very few disadvantages and considerable advantages to inclusion. The more you educate your employees, the better they can do their jobs. How can they know the importance of increasing production efficiency if you haven't told them the consequences of a drop in efficiency? They don't want to hear theoretical hyperbole; they want to know in real terms what a drop in efficiency means for the company's financial health and how that affects them. If a drop in efficiency means there is no money for increased compensation, then tell them that. The days when the boss could demand trust from employees are over. As I said, tell your employees as much as you can, without violating any privacy constraints. Remember, the more an employee knows the better decisions he can make.

All companies face challenges from time to time. Employee involvement in dealing with those challenges can yield real dividends. First, talking to employees about challenges fosters the culture of inclusion. Second, employees often come up with creative ways to meet those challenges—ways you might never have considered. Get your employees involved. There is almost no downside and a potentially great upside.

Consider this: The costs of healthcare in the United States are rising at an alarming rate. Is it better to discuss how these costs affect the company, or simply tell the employees that the company can no longer afford to absorb these rising costs? Which approach has the greatest possibility of yielding the best outcome? These issues are real and require inclusion of employees in the decision-making.

Managing people is a complex matter, as you can see from the topics we have addressed here. However, I know that more than anything else, what is required is treating people fairly and consistently and applying common sense. As a surgeon once told me, "The best malpractice insurance is to take good care of your patients!"

The Importance of Communication

I like to think of effective communication as the process of creating mutual understanding. Looked at in that way, it becomes clear that the whole is indeed greater than the sum of the parts. We have all been in situations where people are talking to each other, but no one seems to be communicating. This results in frustration and heightened emotions. While an actor wants to evoke emotional responses in his audience, a businessman will find that increasing emotions usually have a negative influence on effective communication.

The exception to this is in sales and marketing where emotions are manipulated to increase the impact on the target audience. Outside of that, when people become emotional while discussing a business problem they often stop listening to each other as they strive ever harder to make their points.

Effective communication involves a combination of speaking, listening, reading, and reasoning to foster understanding. It requires a commitment to accomplish something, hopefully for the betterment of the company. This need for commitment cannot be overstated. Without commitment, very little gets accomplished.

Effective communication is generally thought of as the imparting of information. However, communication can also be effective in other areas such as:

- Initiating action
- Establishing a relationship
- Changing attitudes and opinions

In initiating action, the intent is to have one person either direct, cause, or influence another person to undertake a desired action. It can be as simple as getting a simple task accomplished, with a directive such as, "Please enter those parts into the inventory system." Or the task can be more complex: "We need to do a physical inventory of the warehouse." In fact, other than imparting information, in the business world, communication is probably used more for initiating action than for any other purpose. We do this all day long on a small scale and think nothing of it.

Initiating Action

I have learned that we all need to pay more attention to how we request that actions be initiated. We get busy and frequently forget to consider how others perceive our communications. I do this all the time, even though I try not to. There is something to be said for the common courtesies we all learned as children. "Please" and "thank you" may seem unnecessary in the business world. However, they are powerful words precisely because so many business people no longer use them.

I have learned, from my wife, how effectively these words can be used. She never seems to "give orders"; she always makes requests. It is a behavior that could benefit all business managers. So, consider asking for help instead of telling an employee you need his help. Ask an employee to do a task that needs done instead of telling him to do so.

The instant we first meet someone we begin the process of establishing a relationship. Most people try to establish good relationships, as it is generally in their best interest to do so. Perhaps the most important factor in establishing a good working relationship with someone is showing you can listen. Yet it remains one of the most difficult challenges for all of us. Why is that? I think the answer is simple. It is because in a conversation most people are not actively listening, they are simply waiting to respond. Believe me when I say there is a vast difference between listening and waiting to respond. People notice through body language when a person is simply waiting to respond, and they don't like it. This is why you so often feel a conversation was not productive.

Establishing a Relationship

Respect is required for a relationship to be productive. No one really wants to be in any relationship where they feel they are not respected, and we all look for signs of respect. Respect must be demonstrated, not just verbalized. How do you demonstrate that respect? Look back again to your childhood when you were taught an important rule: Do not interrupt others. As we enter adulthood we become convinced that our opinion is vitally important to a discussion and lose sight of that rule. Common courtesy is put on the back burner. I do this; we all do this. Look at the Sunday-morning news programs. It seems that at least half of the time, two or more people are talking at once. No one is being courteous to anyone else, and this behavior has become acceptable. Yet it is so easy to establish respect for the other person by actually listening. Keep in mind that once a person respects you, your ability to influence him or her is greatly enhanced. So, listen carefully and then, and only then, respond.

Changing Attitudes and Opinions

Good communication is required to change another's attitude or opinion. This is more complicated than initiating actions, and requires that you have already established a respectful relationship with the person you are trying to influence. In trying to influence attitudes and opinions, first you must know the desired outcome. Is your intent simply to get someone to see your side of an issue, or are you trying to change an opinion, to get the other person to agree with you? It certainly is much easier to get someone to understand how you see an issue than it is to get someone who is at odds with you to change to agreeing with you. In fact, I don't know how you get someone who fundamentally disagrees with you to change his position without first making sure he understands your position.

Once you have imparted the needed information, in a relationship of mutual respect communication becomes the mechanism to shape opinions and change attitudes. There are thousands of books covering the art of effective communication written by people who have done extensive research into the topic, as it is so complex. However, like most things, I think it usually comes down to just a few basic principles, most of which you were taught in childhood. Add to those principles the necessity to respectfully impart your vision and goals, and you have gone a long way toward influencing others.

Remember that employees are motivated toward achieving a goal or set of goals only when they understand those goals. Without that understanding, it is highly unlikely that employees are really working toward a goal. More than likely they are simply working for pay.

While there is certainly nothing wrong with working for pay, as many people do just that, it does not propel your organization toward improvement or growth. You need employees to fully understand your business goals and get involved in the process. How do you get them involved? By asking them for their input. Get them involved from the beginning, not at the very end. You want to get as many people "inside the tent" as you can and as early as you can.

Communicating with Customers

Employees are only part of the communication challenge facing any company. Customers are the lifeblood of any company; therefore, effective communication with customers is vital. Even though this may seem obvious, I have seen many circumstances in which poor communication cost a company a customer. You can't just deliver a good product or do good work. You must also make sure you are giving your customers what they want in your communication with them. Here are some basic questions to answer:

- Are your customers getting useable information?
- Are you fulfilling your promises?
- Are you promising one thing and delivering something else?

If you are in a service industry, you must keep your customers informed about what services you provide for them, the cost of those services, and when the services will be completed. The company that strives to provide accurate and timely information always has an advantage over the company that fails to do so. Good communication, keeping your customers in the loop, is of real value to them.

Let's say you need to take your car in for servicing. You have a number of choices of where to go. One consideration for you is your perception of the quality of the work performed by each shop that does car repair. If you think that two or more shops provide work of equal quality, don't you always go to the shop where you feel "cared for"? Of course you do; we all do. When you think about what goes into making you feel cared for, timely and accurate communication is a big part of that.

The converse is therefore also true. Customers will become ex-customers if they feel communication is not both timely and proper. Failure to actively and effectively communicate with customers is perhaps the fastest way to lose them. We are all customers at one time or another. The majority of complaints I hear from unhappy customers can be traced back to poor communication practices. This happens to all of us, and we remember those instances longer than we remember good experiences. Simple but true.

General Communication Guidelines

Experts who study the subject will tell you that communication can be grouped into three areas: visual, auditory, and kinesthetic. These are the dominant ways by which we process information.

> Visual—written communication. This includes letters, signs, print media, memos, and so on.

> Auditory—oral communication. This includes conversation, speeches, music, and so on.

> Kinesthetic—physical communication. This includes body language, intonation, energy, sound level, and so on.

When I first learned about the VAK (visual, auditory, kinesthetic) process I found it to be a little complicated. However, the more you think about the basic principles, the more you realize this is exactly what happens as we process information every day. Understanding the VAK process makes us all better communicators.

Visual people need to "see" what you are saying; they want to "see" your goals. They want the vision. Auditory people pay close attention to what they hear and pay less attention to what they see. They often use phrases like, "I hear you." Kinesthetic people focus on body language, dress, energy, motion, and so forth. They want to feel a connection with you.

If you are so inclined, you can improve your communication skills by taking note of whether the person you are communicating with is a visual, auditory, or kinesthetic communicator. I don't spend a great deal of time on this, but I do know the process is valid. A real master of this process does have an advantage in negotiations over someone who does not understand the process at all.

I have read many articles that say the overwhelming majority of people are visual information processors. So that is my default position. Rather than fixating on the VAK process, I try to spend more energy on the basic guidelines listed below. Even though most, if not all of these are obvious, it is amazing how many of these guidelines we regularly ignore. I know I am guilty of that.

Some general guidelines:

- Show respect to whomever you are communicating with. You get what you give.
- Read body language. Is the person you are communicating with comfortable, nervous, distracted, and angry?
- Ask more questions than you give answers. When you ask a question, stop talking and listen.
- Try to keep your questions positive. Negative questions can imply threats or consequences.
- Avoid negative statements. People often feel threatened by negative comments, even if the comment is not directed at them.
- Be an active listener. Be aware of the difference between listening and waiting to respond.
- Always listen for the real (sometimes hidden) message.

- Be aware of the role of perception in the communication process. Perception is reality!
- In written communication get right to the point, and do it clearly. Do not use any unnecessary words.
- When in a situation that involves conflict or potential conflict, ask open-ended questions. This will keep the conversation going and provide you with important information.

Although communication is a very complicated topic, there are ways to break it down into manageable components, as listed above. In my experience, the only way I can continue to communicate in an effective manner is to continually ask myself what the person I am communicating with perceives from me. Am I sending the right message? Am I listening? Am I really being effective?

Communication is undoubtedly the most critical process in effective management. It is not just about getting tasks done. More importantly, it is about sharing with others a vision and goal. You can use effective communication to help your company reach its goals by getting everyone on board with you and functioning as a unit. Being respectful is the starting point, and showing respect for people never ends. Keep in mind, effective communication provides clarity and without clarity (or effective communication) there is confusion.

Conflict Resolution

There is perhaps no more confusing or complicated issue than conflict resolution. Thousands of books and articles have been written on the subject, and there is an expert around every corner. There is no way to completely cover this topic in one chapter, but I do know that most conflicts can be resolved relatively easily if two fundamentals are present. First, all parties must to want to resolve the conflict. Second, all parties must use civility and common sense.

A perfect example of the absence of both of these prerequisites can be seen in the behavior our elected representatives in Washington, DC. There, both sides are posturing for political gain. Neither side is actually trying to resolve differences, nor does civility or common sense ever seem to enter the legislative process. Each side goes to great lengths to create conflict for purely political reasons.

In business, many conflicts result from nothing more than poor communication. So, applying the concepts outlined in the previous chapter on proper communication can often resolve a conflict. Once you have determined that a real conflict exists, and the problem is not simply improper communication, you must ask whether the parties involved are actually seeking a resolution to the situation.

There are certainly times when conflict is used to serve a particular purpose. An example would be a situation in which union leadership incites conflict between the management of a company and the union membership to either instigate a work action or to demonstrate the value the union is delivering to its membership. Certainly, not all labor conflicts occur for these reasons, but you are naïve if you think it doesn't happen. Why? Because unions are composed of people, and we all know people regularly pursue self-interest, even if that pursuit creates conflict. It's unrealistic to pretend this does not happen. Again, just look at our elected representatives in Congress.

On a smaller scale, any individual can also have a hidden agenda that is served by conflict. An obvious example is an employee who is seeking advancement over another employee and uses conflict to further his cause. Again, this is not always the case, but it is unrealistic to pretend it does not happen. It does happen, and you should simply recognize that fact. These are just two examples of conflicts that do not meet the first criteria for resolution: all parties seeking a resolution. We can all think of many more examples, but I see no need to expound further. Just be aware that there may be hidden agendas in a conflict in which case one or more parties may not be honestly seeking a resolution.

Once you have determined that the parties in conflict are looking for a resolution, you can start dealing with the problem using civility and common sense, using some basic principles that have helped me deal with conflict. They are:

- Concentrate on the problem, not the person—in other words, don't shoot the messenger.
- Concentrate on what people need, not on their stated positions.
- Look first for areas of agreement—this is always the best place to start.
- Make sure any agreements are clear and fully understood by all parties.

By concentrating on the problem that needs resolving you avoid the danger of looking for someone to blame or to punish. People naturally get very emotional when they feel in any way threatened. Not personalizing the problem can go a long way toward keeping the discussion on an intellectual level, not an emotional level.

For example, a customer complains to you that she is not getting timely information on the status of a big job you are doing for her company. You go to your department manager with the problem and ask what is happening. The manager acknowledges that he has been slow in getting information to customers. You chastise the manager for being unresponsive. That will certainly create animosity between you and your manager and probably between your manager and the customer. No resolution here.

You could concentrate on the problem, rather than the person, by asking your manager what is keeping him from communicating more frequently with the customer. More than likely he will say he is so busy that he simply doesn't have time to respond, even though he fully understands that he should respond. So is the problem with him, or do you have a structural problem in your company? Further investigation may show you that if you only took one or two minor responsibilities off of his plate, he would then have time to communicate more fully with customers. In that case the problem is not with the person; it is with the structure. You can avoid the tendency to blame by concentrating on the problem, not on the person.

Once both you and your manager realize that the problem is with the company structure, your manager may well tell you that if he doesn't get more help his department will not meet production goals. He is unyielding about this problem and insistent that the only means of solving the problem is to hire additional employees. But what if you do not have money in your budget to hire additional people? Now you and your manager are at odds. He insists that he must have more people. You do not have the money to hire more people. Sounds like a rather common conflict to me. What happens now? Do you proceed from the standpoint of his stated position and therefore stay at odds with him? You could, but that will most likely result in growing resentment on the part of both you and your manager.

Another way to look at this is to realize that all the manager is really saying to you is that he has a problem, is aware of the problem, and has tendered a solution. In his mind, he has thought the problem through and come to the only reasonable conclusion. He needs more help, or he can't do what he needs (and wants) to do. These things occur in business on a daily basis. So, concentrate on the company need, not the manager's unwavering position. Could you reassign tasks from another employee to assist him in some way? Could technology help? Would time management training help? Concentrate on the need, not the stated position.

Not all issues are easily resolved by concentrating on the problem or the need. I have found that conflicts that are not resolved by either of these first two techniques often break down into two categories: those that are more complex and so cannot be easily resolved; and those that simply cannot be resolved to everyone's satisfaction. Assuming the latter, an employee may come to you and say he has accepted a position at a competitor's business. The job is much closer to home for him, he has better hours so will have more family time, and he is getting a substantial increase in pay. In this case, it is simply better to wish him well than to try to change his mind. The deck is stacked against you here. Unless you are going to offer him your job, you are destined to lose him. This is where you admit that not all conflicts are resolvable to everyone's satisfaction.

One example of a complex conflict that can be resolved is a contract or agreement negotiation. Generally your negotiation will be with a union, a vendor, or a service provider. All union contracts are complex by their very nature. If you are engaging the services of a vendor to construct a building for you, those negotiations are also complex. The same is true if you are engaging a software company to overhaul your company's IT systems. These are complex issues that take patience, willingness to compromise, and a commitment to reach a resolution that is acceptable to all.

In any negotiation I like to first look for any points of agreement. That sets a good tone for subsequent discussions. It shows a willingness to work with the other party and leads to a stronger relationship throughout the remainder of your discussions. The more you can agree on in the very beginning, the more that momentum can be of help in getting you through the process.

Most of these negotiations will eventually come down to an agreement on money. Money discussions are also often a value judgment where both sides are weighing the money offered against their perceived value for that money. Notice I said perceived value. To increase the perceived value in the minds of the other entity (the union, builder, vendor, etc.), get as many easy points agreed upon as early as you can. Seasoned diplomats in complex international negotiations commonly use this tactic.

One helpful technique is to ask yourself if you are continually trying to improve the situation. Does the point you are currently discussing get you closer to an agreement? Don't take an unwavering position on a point that is minor at best and doesn't really get you closer to an agreement. You can't give away the farm on minor points, which is why they are minor points. Keep your eye on the big picture. Establish give and take. Keep your ego in check. In fact, check your ego at the front door; it never serves you well in trying to resolve conflicts or negotiate solutions. I have seen too many instances where resolutions seemed to be just around the corner only to be derailed by someone being unable to control his ego. Negotiations then fall apart, and everyone loses.

How does this happen? It is generally because someone takes the parochial viewpoint: "If I am right, you must be wrong!" Looked at another way, one person may refuse to recognize the validity of the other person's viewpoint, because if the other person's viewpoint is correct, that must mean his or her viewpoint is wrong. I have seen this play out quite often.

Women are generally much better at checking their egos than men. That is why I have always sought the opinions of women in conflict resolution. It has served me well. Just remember, ego is always a stumbling block to an agreement.

People are often unsure about how to get conflict resolution or negotiations moving toward a positive result. I know I have had problems with this issue in the past. What I have learned is so fundamental, it almost seems too simple to work. The best way to get things moving is to ask nonthreatening questions, and listen to the answers. Then follow up those answers with more positive questions, and so on.

I know this sounds too good to be true. However, one of the best negotiators I have ever seen did exactly this. He had in his mind the result he wanted but always directed the conversations by asking a series of questions. All of his questions were designed to keep the conversations going. He also peppered the questions with comments that highlighted areas of agreement. Before too long the resolution would often be obvious to all parties, and all parties felt they had significant input into the resolution, since they did.

Below, I list some examples of basic questions and statements you can use, but you should always try to personalize them to your specific situation and use them in an order that is appropriate for the circumstances.

To get or keep the conversation going ask:

1. What is your primary concern?
2. How has this affected you?
3. What would you like to do?
4. What do you see as the best solution?

5. How does that resolve the problem?
6. What are you trying to accomplish?
7. Who else have you spoken with about this, and what did he or she tell you?
8. Tell me what has upset you.

When responding to resistance, ask or say:

1. Well, what would happen if we did that?
2. I can see your point. I don't know, but that might work.
3. That's a very good point. Are there any other options?
4. OK, but what would happen if we did that?
5. I see, but help me understand how that makes it better.
6. Should we consider anything else?
7. What do you see as the most viable option?
8. Well, that's certainly an option. Do we have any other options?

None of these are particularly elegant, which is precisely why I like them. They are simple. They are straightforward. They are understandable. In order for this approach to work, you must receive and fully understand the viewpoint of the other parties in the negotiation. These questions and statements encourage people to share their viewpoints. Once you think you understand the other person's position, make sure you restate that understanding to them. Do not assume your understanding is complete without restating it to them.

This is where you recap whatever agreement has been reached; making sure it is clear to everyone and fully understood. I can't stress this too much. Take the time to reiterate what has been agreed upon. You might even need to put that agreement in writing (especially for union and service contracts). I can't tell you how many times I made assumptions about agreement that were not the same as the other person's assumptions about the same agreement. It sometimes seems unnecessary to reiterate what you think is obvious, but it is never a waste of time.

As I said earlier, this is a complex topic. There is no one best way to approach the solutions. You will not be able to resolve all conflicts, even though you try your best. Do not fixate on being perfect in resolving conflicts. Do the best you can by being civil, considerate, and using common sense.

Leadership Principles

"Leadership is the ability to affect change."
—M.D. Lacey

This is a definition of leadership that I really like, because it only deals with how a leader affects the people around him or her, without making moral or ethical value judgments. This definition does not deal with right and wrong, good and bad, left and right, up and down, or any other way you make a judgment of values.

Certainly, value judgments exist and always will. However, what I am discussing here is how a leader affects the people around him or her. So, instead of talking about good or bad, I am talking about being effective or ineffective. Nor am I talking about motivating people. I am not a believer in the long-term value of external motivation. If you have someone in your group who constantly needs outside motivation, then you probably have an underperforming person whose value to your organization is questionable.

Leaders are constantly being evaluated by those around them. If you pay close attention to what is being said about a group's leader, the comments generally revolve around some common areas: communication skills, people management, time management, and delegation of tasks. We all look for effectiveness in each of these areas in making determinations about who is and who is not a strong leader. The more effective you are in these areas, the stronger your leadership becomes.

To be an effective leader, you must practice good communication skills. Being a good communicator may be the most important aspect of effective leadership. As I think about the characteristics that are present in effective leaders, I can't think of anything more important than communication. Look at leaders like Ronald Reagan, Bill Clinton, Margaret Thatcher, and John Kennedy, and you will see prime examples of leaders who clearly understood the power of communication. Since communication has already been discussed in a previous chapter, I will not cover it again. Just keep in mind that the intent of communication is to make a connection. Once you have made a connection, you are half way to effectively influencing others.

Beyond communication here are four critical areas of effective leadership:

- Recruiting people
- Managing people
- Delegating tasks
- Managing yourself

Recruiting People: Some General Guidelines

One of the most critical challenges facing any leader is recruiting the right people. I believe a weak leader likes to surround himself with people he believes he can dominate. My advice is to do just the opposite. Try to recruit people who are more intelligent than you, or more experienced than you, or both. Your company will benefit for years to come from this practice.

There is also a great deal of value to any organization when people have diversity of thought and are actively encouraged to express that diversity.

FUNDAMENTALS OF BUSINESS

Without a free and vigorous discussion of important issues you usually end up with poor decisions and an underperforming organization. Why is that? Because there is real risk involved when one person makes all the key decisions without a full understanding of opposing viewpoints. Every strong leader wants and needs checks and balances. No one knows it all; so don't pretend that you do. Hire good people, give them free rein to express their opinions, and by doing so you will collectively make better decisions. I agree with this quote from Jack Welch, "The team with the best players wins!" But there is a caveat here that cannot be ignored.

Recruiting strong people and encouraging them to freely express themselves can create another problem, if not dealt with properly. That issue is lack of adherence to decisions. This can arise when it is not clear to your team that although you want each member to freely state his or her opinion on topics during the discussion process, once a decision is made everyone must fully support that decision. It is very easy for team members to get caught up in the emotions of a heated discussion, fail to recognize that a decision has been made, and therefore that it is now time to move forward with the decision. This can cause unnecessary turmoil in any organization. The more strongly someone feels about a topic, the more it is important to emphasize that although discussion is vital, once a decision is made there is no place for dissent.

When you hire strong people you must also make sure they are properly placed within your company. So you not only have the right people but you also have them positioned correctly. In his book *Good to Great*, Jim Collins made this point very well. This is certainly a major challenge to all leaders and is one of the reasons that professional sports teams are constantly shuffling players from one team to another. It is not only about getting the most talented players, it is also about asking yourself, "Of the available talented players, which one fills the need we have most on our team right now?" Once you have assembled a strong team, the real challenge begins, and getting the most from your team is a never-ending challenge.

Managing People: Some General Guidelines

The best advice I can give anyone starting in a leadership role is to listen, listen, and listen. Without question, I have learned more about management skills by listening to knowledgeable people than from all of the books I have read, courses I have taken, or business seminars I have attended. Whether this means I am a slow learner or just retained more from listening is an interesting proposition. However, I do believe I am of reasonable intelligence, so I am going with listening as simply being more valuable to me.

We have already dealt with good listening skills in the chapter on communication, so refer to that chapter if you need more on this. Remember, there is a real difference between hearing and listening. Good listening is an attempt to understand what is being communicated. Also remember that communication can be nonverbal as well as verbal. Pay attention to both.

I was once in an office of a supplier of my company. I had an appointment to meet with the company vice president. I had spoken with him on the telephone many times, but had never met him. When I entered his office, the man was seated behind a very large wooden desk. In front of his desk were two chairs for visitors. The interesting thing about those chairs was that they were small and somewhat low to the floor. So once you sat down in a chair, you were looking up at the vice president. More importantly, he was looking down at you. Since the chairs were small, they were also uncomfortable. This was his way to establishing control of the situation. I should have asked him if he had those chairs brought in for special occasions or did everyone who came into his office have to sit on them. Anyway, he was clearly trying to make a point about who was in control of the meeting. While I find this technique to be a bit crude, it was effective.

Beyond communication, your main responsibility as a leader is to communicate to your team your vision of where your company is headed. Employees invest themselves, their futures, and their family's futures into the company. It is only natural that they would want to know that they have a future and what that future may look like. You do not need to gather all your employees together and make a speech. In fact, I can't remember ever doing that. I find it to be much more effective to have small meetings or one-on-one conversations with employees. It is keeping the conversation going that is critical and that can be accomplished in more than one way.

Sharing information is a critical part of sharing a vision. You can't just tell people what you think the future is for the company. If you want to be effective, you must tell them why you see things the way you do. If you do not provide any information to support your vision, your employees will get suspicious and nervous. Wouldn't you? If they can't understand your vision, they will never accept it. Since it is always best to have a united team, tell them as much as you can about what really matters to them—the future of the company.

I have spoken with many business owners and leaders whose philosophy was, "What they don't know won't hurt them." To me, that philosophy is doomed to failure from the outset. If your business is struggling because production costs are too high to provide you the necessary margin, then let your team know. If you really need to increase your pricing but are reluctant to do so, tell your team and see what they say. Getting the issues on the table, seeing them for what they are, and asking for input is important to long-term success. If your team is committed to their future in the company, you will most often get useful feedback. I have never understood the concept of keeping everything about the company a secret from the employees. Who cares more about the success of a company than the people who make their livelihood working there?

I have also heard the retort, "They won't understand what I am talking about!" I see this as shirking a leader's responsibility. It is nothing more than a way of saying that you would need to put some thought, time, and effort into explaining the business environment to the employees, and you really can't be bothered to do so. That is not leadership.

So, educate your employees on your business. You will find that people are not stupid; they simply need educating. Let's say you own a construction company. Do you know how to plumb a house? Can you run all the electrical wiring? Can you do all the finish carpentry work? Probably not, but with the proper education you might be able to. At the very least, you would understand the fundamentals of what needs to be done. The same holds true for your employees. They may not be able to assume your position in the company, but educating them will help them understand the challenges the company is facing.

Certainly you will need to tailor your information to the audience, as is true in most any situation. You would spend much more time on financial details if you were speaking to a chief financial officer than if you were speaking to a mechanic or a salesman. It also follows that you would spend more time on customer acquisition and retention if you were speaking to the marketing team than you would if you were speaking to a room of accountants. It is your responsibility to connect with your team. Failure to do so usually has dire consequences, such as lost productivity, high turnover, and poor quality products. Any of these can destroy your company.

Don't expect your team to always come to you to start the dialogue. Get in the habit of going to them. Time and time again I have seen people in leadership blissfully going along with their daily work while problems are brewing in their organization. When a problem finally surfaces, as it always does, and I ask the leader what caused the problem, a common response is, "I don't really know. No one said anything to me." That shows me that the leader is not actively communicating; he is passively communicating. Waiting for your team to come to you, because you are too busy, does not work. Find the time to meet with them. It is worth it.

If you have established a pattern of providing information to your employees, then you have started the process of establishing your own legitimacy. If your team members are to get behind your vision, they must see you as a legitimate leader. You cannot inherit legitimacy; it must be earned. You can earn it by educating your team, asking many questions, listening closely to the responses, and showing respect at all times. Relate to people in ways that are most important to them and provide information they can understand. That is when you are speaking their language.

Most leaders spend far too much time thinking about whether or not they are getting the proper respect from their team. What a waste of time. First of all, like legitimacy, respect is earned. It does not automatically come with the assumption of a leadership position. It is up to you to establish a foundation of mutual respect with your team.

For a leader to be respected by his or her team, he or she must first show respect to the team. This should not be too difficult to understand. Yet, so many leaders get it backward, wanting respect from the team first. One of the reasons they do is the failure to understand that there is a difference between showing respect for the position and actually respecting the person holding that position. Respect for the position should be automatically given, out of common courtesy. That is a fundamental tenet of a functional society. Think of the practice of everyone rising when a judge enters a courtroom. This is done out of respect for the position, not necessarily for the person. Respect for the person is generally withheld until he or she has shown that respect is deserved.

There are various ways to earn respect. This means there is no one 'right' way. As I said, the first step in earning personal respect is to show personal respect. People look to leadership for answers in times of difficulty and that presents an opportunity for any leader. The effective leader tries to avoid solutions with there are clear winners and losers. That is not always possible, but it is obviously preferable. So, strive to avoid having clear-cut winners and losers. The leader who spends some time probing the situation, asking questions, can produce insights that help solve problems in such a way as to provide something for everyone. This ability to avoid a losing situation while searching for a solution will go a long way to getting your team behind you.

The Socratic Method—asking questions then stating your understanding of the responses—is important in letting team members know you are interested in their viewpoints. That is your way of showing them respect. Also, by reiterating your understanding of their viewpoints back to them, you give them the opportunity to correct misunderstandings on your part. Finally, it will frequently lead them to arrive at the same conclusions you have drawn from the discussion. It is a learning opportunity for everyone.

There cannot always be a "win" for everyone. Frequently, you will need to make decisions with which someone will be unhappy. That's OK. Just make sure all your employees know they were included in the decision-making process and understand how that process was conducted. Remember, it is important to keep your team inside the tent looking out, not outside the tent looking in. It is the effort you show here that will earn you respect from your team members. They must feel included.

A quick note here about the difference between respect and trust. First, they are not the same. While I can certainly trust an electrician to do a job properly, that does not mean I respect him as a person. I can trust a banker to wire funds for me, but that does not mean I respect her. We frequently interact with people we trust to do something, but do not necessarily respect. If you are to be an effective team leader, you need both trust and respect. At least, that is ideal. People want to be able to both trust that you have the best interests of the team at heart and also respect you as you make difficult decisions. To show an employee that he can place his trust in you, first you must demonstrate a level of competence in what you are doing or providing for that person. Beyond that, people must also be able to trust your truthfulness and sincerity. In this, they are making a value judgment about you. In a leadership situation, with diversity of thought, trust outweighs respect.

It is one thing to clearly explain your vision to your team members and quite another to get them to line up behind that vision. Nowhere is this more clearly demonstrated in our national political environment. It certainly is not the case that one political party does not understand the position of the other; they just do not line up behind the other's position. In order to get your team members to line up behind your vision, you must win them over by establishing both trust and respect. This is an ongoing process. It has no endpoint. So, how do you get your team members involved in the process?

Involvement

Generally speaking people will only become involved in a situation if they feel they can influence the process and have a stake in the outcome. Ask yourself this question, "What person is going to become involved in a situation with neither skin in the game nor influence in the outcome?" It takes energy to become involved in any situation. Anyone willing to expend that energy must have a stake in the outcome. However, giving people a stake in the outcome is only one part of getting your team involved in the process.

When you're taking a flight from one city to another certainly you have a stake in the outcome—a very important stake. But, the typical passenger has very little ability to influence the outcome. It is that ability to influence the outcome that motivates people to expend the time and energy to become involved in the process. I find it very interesting to board a flight and see how many of my fellow passengers are very nervous about flying. The truth is, the plane will either land safely or not, and as a passenger there is not much you can do to influence the landing. That is why seasoned travelers show very little excitement about flying. It is not that they do not have a stake in the outcome; it is that they realize that they have very little influence over the outcome.

People can get very excited and energized about issues over which they believe they have direct influence. Being able to influence an outcome, through involvement in a process, therefore has the potential to either help or harm them within the organization. When people feel they have influence over an outcome they take ownership for their involvement in the process and the outcomes that ensue. With this ownership comes accountability for the result. But many people are reluctant to be accountable for the result. It either frightens them or just makes them uncomfortable.

This ownership has to do with personal responsibility (accountability). A good and valuable team member will not shy away from taking personal responsibility for outcomes. These people are your future leaders. They are willing to hold themselves accountable, and that is a trait you want to foster.

You must also give your employees some authority. You cannot hold an employee responsible for an outcome if you have not given him the authority to do what he needs to do to accomplish that outcome. I know this seems almost elementary, but I have seen many situations where a team member was held responsible for an outcome without ever being empowered to do what was necessary. That is a failure of leadership on the part of the supervisor.

When people are not empowered to do what needs to be done they do not feel any responsibility for the outcome. How could they? Why would you expect them to? They may express regret for failing to meet a goal, but that expression of regret does not mean they actually feel responsible. Do not mistake one for the other. People only feel responsible when they have both the backing of the leader and the authority to get things done. Someone may be a passenger on the plane, but unless he or she is the pilot it is not the passenger's fault if the plane crashes. Of course this is of little consolation to the individual and the other passengers.

Empowerment

Empowerment is also important for employee involvement. I have always tried to empower team members to fix what needs to be fixed. They do not need my authorization to right a wrong or to correct a mistake. If they need my permission for every task, no matter how small, then I am micromanaging them, and that is wasteful. If you have to micromanage an employee, then why does the team need him? Teach your employees to be thoughtful, thorough, and respectful of lines of authority, while also empowering them to correct problems. If you never put team members in a leadership position and force them to make tough decisions, how can you expect them to become leaders?

I once worked for a man I was convinced was a "natural born" leader. He just seemed to know how to handle people and instinctively analyze situations. In fact, he was so quick to analyze situations it was intimidating. I was amazed at his abilities and was certain he had to be born with them. He wasn't. In observing him I realized what he did very well was ask questions, listen to responses, and figure out how he could get others involved in solving problems. In analyzing what he was doing, I also discovered a real shortcoming. He was reluctant to empower team members to fix problems. That one shortcoming left everyone with a feeling of uncertainty about his decisions, which in turn led to team members being reluctant to make decisions. This can be a real problem for a company, since it can lead to no one being willing to makes necessary decisions. Therefore, time is wasted and progress slows.

Finally, by definition, every team member is involved in whatever the team is doing. However, personal involvement goes beyond that. If you want a high-performing team, the individuals on that team must be personally involved in its performance. That personal involvement comes from having a stake in the outcome, an ability to influence the situation, an understanding of accountability, and an empowerment to act. Otherwise, the team members are all just riders on the bus, and, though they may see and understand your vision for the company, they are not actively supporting that vision.

Resistance

This is an issue every leader must deal with at one time or another. You should expect to encounter resistance. It will happen. It is a part of the process and is not always a negative. Understanding the basics of resistance is critical in helping you deal with it.

I have heard resistance defined as "diversity of thought." If you think of resistance in this manner, then you will not automatically be against it. However, I think we all know there is more than one type of resistance. There is resistance that is constructive and resistance that is not constructive. You should encourage constructive resistance while at the same time insisting on respect for individuals and common courtesies.

If resistance is diversity of thought and that diversity is directed toward solving problems or furthering the goals of the company, then it is constructive. Encourage that. Do not encourage resistance that furthers the goals of an individual but does not further company goals. It may take some educating to make the person see how his position is not constructive. With a strong team member and patience on your part, you should be able to effectively mentor him on this. If you are unable to do that, you might have the wrong person on the team. Be honest here. If you have the wrong person on the team, get that person off the team.

Why do you want to foster diversity of thought? Diversity is the breeding ground for creativity. Creativity is one of the forces that propels organizations forward. An organization without creativity is relegated to keep doing things the way they have always been done. There is no room for growth in that approach. You also end up as a living proof of Einstein's definition of insanity: "...doing the same thing over and over again and expecting different results." I have seen too many companies do this. Remember, if you suppress constructive resistance, you may also be suppressing creativity, which can't be good.

Since resistance is a feeling, not a fact, in dealing with it you will be dealing with how people feel about certain situations as opposed to the facts about the situations. Facts may be used to support a person's feeling about a specific issue, but those facts are not what are generally in dispute. It is the conclusions drawn from the facts that create resistance in an organization. Notwithstanding those individuals who seem to be resistant to everything, resistance can generally be traced back to a misunderstanding of the facts or a mismatch of the conclusions drawn from those facts.

Therefore, a complete understanding of the facts involved in any specific issue is important, along with an agreement on the facts. Take the time to articulate the facts, and make sure there is a consensus as to the facts themselves. Your challenge is to align conclusions drawn from those facts with the goals of the organization.

People will use their own history and value systems in evaluating facts and drawing conclusions. This is why I have said that resistance is a feeling, not a fact. This is to be expected. It is your ability to align those conclusions with the goals of the organization that will enable you to effectively deal with any resistance you encounter. So, always start with the facts and then try to align people's conclusions with the needs of the organization.

Dealing with conclusions drawn from a set of facts is personal in nature and is based on the value system of the person or persons drawing the conclusion. If you have done a good job articulating your company's goals and values, it should be relatively straightforward to align conclusions drawn from facts with those goals. This is to say, if the facts are not in doubt but the conclusion is, your challenge is to change the perception of the individual drawing other conclusions from those facts. Remember, an individual's perception is his reality, and it is that reality you must address.

What you are trying to achieve here is the unity within the organization and agreement on how to proceed. By aligning the values of your team members with the goals of the organization, you have a much better opportunity to achieve the organizational goals. However, this requires a willingness to listen to the issues being raised along with an ability to understand their meaning and show appreciation for other's input into the process. You are looking for unity in how to proceed, not an elimination of diverse viewpoints.

If you demonstrate that you are open to diverse viewpoints, you will get those diverse viewpoints. However, this carries with it the willingness to open yourself up to second-guessing. That's part of the process, and your willingness to be wrong will greatly influence your team's willingness to be wrong. You cannot ever say, "I told you so." That will kill future openness. So, listen carefully, encourage openness, align the goals of the individual with the goals of the organization, and encourage a willingness to take chances by making constructive suggestions.

Delegation of Tasks

By delegating tasks you can help your team members learn and grow. This growth is critical to the overall performance of your organization. If you do not assign new tasks to your employees, they will become complacent. If they never have anything new to challenge them, they will become bored. So, your willingness to delegate is important to company growth.

There is certainly not just one way to delegate tasks to your team. But, there are some basics that can be used in the delegation process. First, if a task can be delegated, you should make every effort to do so. There may be many tasks you could keep for yourself, but why would you do so? If you are actively trying to educate your younger team members, then use the delegation process to assist in their education. This will also free you up to spend more time on other projects and long-term planning.

Do not delegate tasks without setting goals and expectations. The goal is what is to be achieved by the task: the desired result. The expectations involve communication of issues or concerns and a time frame for completing the tasks being delegated. If issues arise, and they almost always do, communication of those issues back to you is very important to make sure the goal is achieved. It is not that unusual for a task to be delegated, with a goal and a time frame, only to discover at the designated time of completion that a problem was encountered and the process stagnated. All too often I have awaited a result only to learn that a problem had been encountered but not communicated. This can be avoided by insisting on timely communication of all problems encountered in the task, which brings me to the next tenet of delegation.

Always check on the progress of the delegated tasks. If I am expecting a result from a delegated task, it is my responsibility to check on the progress being made. If I fail to do so, that is my mistake, and I have only myself to blame.

Before you assign a task, make sure the resources required to complete the task have been provided. These resources also include the authority needed to successfully complete the assigned task. Think the process through carefully. What would you need to be able to complete the task? Are you providing those resources to the people you assigned to the task?

Do not make assumptions about knowledge. It is very dangerous to simply assume that all team members know how to do what you are asking them to do. Go through the components of what is involved in completing the task. Ask questions to find out how much your team members understand. Assume nothing. Remember, when assigned an important task, many people find it even more difficult to speak up and ask for more information or help. They may see it as a poor reflection on themselves, and may be very sensitive to anything that reflects poorly on them. So, before handing off a task, make sure that everyone fully understands the components of the task. Avoid a situation in which you might end up saying, "I just assumed they knew that!"

Along with the resources and authority to complete the task comes accountability for the results. If you never hold people accountable for results, they cannot learn what it is to assume higher and higher levels of responsibility within your company. This is like giving every kid playing on a team a trophy for participation regardless of how the team did. That does not happen in the business world. So, hold your team accountable for achieving the goals for all delegated tasks. Employees will learn responsibility to the team and be better positioned to grow within the company. Requiring accountability pays off.

Finally, strive to delegate the tasks that you like to do the most. Why would you do that? Aren't those the tasks you should keep for yourself? Well, they certainly are the tasks you want to keep for yourself. However, if you delegate them, you will naturally be more inclined to keep track of their progress since you do like doing them. Delegating what you do not like to do is a very common mistake, so do just the opposite. It can be difficult because it means you are keeping the tasks you don't really like doing. Bite the bullet; your company will benefit if you do.

Managing Yourself

Managing yourself can be more challenging than managing your team. If you are already successful in business, it is very easy to become complacent about your managerial habits. You can become lackadaisical with yourself as you focus on managing your team, planning for future success, and meeting current and future challenges. Add to this the possibility that some members of your team may remain reluctant to challenge you (notwithstanding everything you have done to foster openness and diversity of thought), and it is likely that you need to occasionally take stock of yourself. I find this to be true in my case since I know that I make more mistakes than I should. By reviewing yourself and your work habits, you can find and correct mistakes and thereby improve the performance of your company. Two areas to look at are how you manage your time and how well you function as a leader. We will take a closer look at both time management and leadership analysis in the next two sections.

Time Management

Efficient use of time is one of the most critical skills any busy executive can learn. So much time is wasted each day by concentrating efforts on nonproductive tasks. It then becomes very important to master the concept of effective time management. I recommend that all employees start using time management skills. Any tool that will increase efficiency should be carefully considered.

One of the most useful tools I have come across in effective time management is the four-quadrant process. It is easy to understand and also easy to implement. I take no credit for devising this process and actually cannot remember when I was first exposed to it. This process was first credited to US President Dwight Eisenhower. However, Dr. Stephen Covey popularized it in his book *Seven Habits of Highly Effective People*.

To implement this process, you classify what you are working on in terms of its overall importance to the company. All of your tasks are classified into one of four quadrants, as shown below.

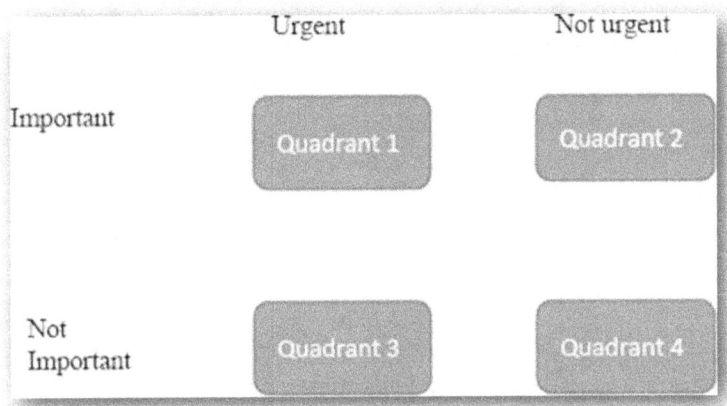

Quadrant one is for tasks that are both urgent and important. I call this the fireman's quadrant. If it is both urgent and important, it is akin to putting out a fire. It must be worked on immediately, just as soon as you can get to it.

We all know people who seem to never stop putting out fires. Doing so can be addictive because it carries with it a feeling of importance and a sense of immediate accomplishment. These are also the same people who constantly complain that they cannot get anything of substance accomplished.

People who live in quadrant one never become planners and do not seem to have time to see the long-term view, much less work on it. They are always frustrated and have a high burnout rate due to stress. However, it is paradoxical that the reason they live in quadrant one is because they do not force themselves to do long-term planning. Since they do not have an executable plan, they are always being reactive. Hence, they never stop putting out fires.

Quadrant two is for items that are important but not urgent. This is where you do your short-term and long-range planning. Your goal should be to spend the majority of your time on issues that fit into this quadrant. Doing so allows you to avoid living in quadrant one, where you're always putting out fires, and to make long-term plans for the success of your company. By spending your time in quadrant two, you are prioritizing the items that have the most value for your company. It also gives you time to adjust to changes in your environment.

I am a strong believer in active planning as the key to long-term success. By making sure you are spending your time in pursuit of issues that are important but not urgent (quadrant two), you are devoting your time to planning for your own success.

Quadrants three and four are where the majority of time is wasted. You must ask yourself, why would you spend any time on pursuits that are not important? If what you're doing is not important, then does it not also follow that spending your time on that task is by definition a waste of time? I see items that fall into quadrant three as "busy work." I have never seen any busy work yield positive results.

Quadrant four is a complete waste of time. People who spend time in this quadrant are frequently surfing the Internet instead of doing valuable and necessary tasks. If you are a busy executive, you simply cannot afford to spend any time in pursuits that are both not important and not urgent.

Aside from the four-quadrant process, you can develop specific habits to help with effective time management. I am not a believer in a long list of "dos and don'ts," because I think you spend more time making sure you are in compliance with the list than you do executing tasks. This is obviously not what you want to do. However, there are some basic guidelines you can follow that will improve your use of time. Here is a short list:

- Schedule meetings in the morning before everyone's day gets busy. Morning meetings are always more productive than afternoon meetings, though "afternoon people" will disagree with this.
- If you need more time in your workday, add it to the morning. Most people are simply more productive in the morning, and you will get more done than if you add the time to the end of the day.
- Keep an ongoing "To Do" list. I prefer the manual method of pen and paper, but there are many ways to do this. Many software programs such as MS Outlook and QuickBooks include task lists. Your cell phone should have an app for such a list. Use whatever you want. Just make sure you have one.
- While I encourage an open door policy, that does not mean you need a steady stream of people in your office. Do not attend or convene meetings that do not have a defined purpose. When a meeting starts, be sure to ask, "What are we trying to accomplish here?"
- Keep control of the flow of meetings. Attempt to foster open discussion while at the same time staying on topic. This requires a degree of discretion in keeping discussions going without letting people ramble. Good facilitation skills are helpful here.
- If you are really pressed for time, then be sure to ask yourself, "Is what I am currently working on really important?"

I would just like to make a couple of other points regarding effective use of your time. First, you must be willing to say no to requests for your time. You can't always do this, as it sends a message of noncommunication. However, when you need to say no, you should do so. If you are always immediately available, then you will always be interrupted. It only takes a short amount of time for your team to become more efficient and selective in the requests they make for your time. Remember that your team members are busy also, and you can help them more efficiently use their time by showing them how to do so.

Second, keep in mind the social protocol in making and receiving a phone call. It is socially accepted that the person initiating the phone call owns the right to terminate the call. So if you are busy when your phone rings and need to let the person calling you leave a message, then you become the person who has control over the length of the return phone call. This can save you a great deal of time when used effectively, yet courteously. Do not be a fanatic about this, as it can create other problems. For example, many years ago a vendor with whom I did business hired an efficiency expert to improve his operation. Within a week of his getting this "expert" assistance, it became nearly impossible to reach anybody at the vendor's company. When I would call and ask to speak with someone the standard response was, "He's in a meeting. Can I take a message and have him get back to you?" This became extremely irritating and caused conflict between my company and the vendor. We could never get anyone on the phone when we called. I knew that I could not be the only person experiencing this. Eventually I was forced to tell the vendor's president that if this kept up I would have to switch vendors. This is a perfect example of taking time management efficiency to the extreme and not taking into account the importance of customer service.

Even so, do not give out your personal phone numbers to business acquaintances. By doing so, you give them permission to call you at all hours of the day and night. If you are unavailable when the person calls (and there are many reasons you would not be immediately available), then you have just created the opposite of the effect you intended. This may seem unfair, but it is true. Someone who has your phone number and calls you expects you to answer. When you don't answer, you have created a small point of tension that could have been avoided by simply not giving out your personal information. Here you are trying to be more available to your customers, and now one of them is irritated at you because you did not answer his phone call late in the evening. This creates an interesting paradox.

Third, do what you least like to do first. Putting it off, because you do not want to do it, is natural. Don't pretend it isn't. Force yourself to put unpleasant tasks at the top of your list. The sooner you do them, the better off you will be. I use this guideline for all tasks, business or personal. It helps with productivity and lessens any stress associated with undesirable tasks.

These are some guidelines that can help you be more effective in the use of your time. You cannot immediately implement them all. Some you will never implement. That is OK. I really don't believe in fanatical time management. I know some people who do, but I have seen too many situations in which a fanatical approach to time management has cost the company in other areas. If there were just one habit I would recommend more than any other, it would be to use the four-quadrant process. It is simple and easy and will save a great deal of time.

Leadership Analysis

> "Leaders do the right thing. Managers do things right."
> —Warren G. Bennis
> American Scholar
> 1925 - 2014

Taking stock of yourself is important for your continued professional growth and the growth of your company. What do you do well? Where do you need to improve? We all have areas of strong performance and weak performance. Knowing your strengths and weaknesses is the first step to ongoing improvement—nothing earth shattering is revealed here.

There are many formal surveys available to help with this, and I am certain a human resources specialist would recommend this type of approach. However, I believe it is more valuable to engage in self-analysis while soliciting input from your team. The question then becomes, "Are you paying attention to the information you are getting?" You could think of information as an equalizer, a way of putting you and your employees on a more equal footing. This is when the flow of information becomes very helpful. The continual flow of useful information helps you prepare for the future. Without it, you are at a disadvantage.

Where do you get useful information? You get it from the members of your team. If you really pay attention to what is said to you, you can get a good understanding of how your team members see you as a leader. This information usually comes in the form of casual comments and is often humorous. Humor allows your team to tell you something without feeling threatened. I have learned to pay attention to these comments and have found them to be valuable. It can also be more formal, as when someone wants to meet with you to discuss a concern. But, such formal requests are generally less common than the informal casual comments.

I once worked with someone who was nicknamed "Chihuahua." He was given that nickname at a previous workplace because he was seen as a person who was always barking at his team. I'm quite sure he remains unaware of this moniker even though it has traveled with him. He was never known as someone who paid close attention to the opinions of others. This was too bad for him, as he was really a very talented manager in most other ways.

I have already discussed many of the obvious characteristics of an effective leader: providing as vision for your company; communicating effectively; having a plan for success; and managing people effectively. If you were thinking that there must be more to it than that, you would be correct. As we all know, leadership is another subject on which many books have been written, many studies have been done, and a wide variety of opinions exist. In self-analysis, I will only address some basic ideas beyond what has already been addressed. Although these ideas may be basic, they are still very important.

Clarity

Bringing clarity to a situation is an important skill for a leader to have. Staying unemotional and detached from personal biases is vital to bringing clarity. Any organization, whether it is a company or a baseball team, is made up of people who have emotions and feel personally involved in the situations in which they find themselves. People's emotions greatly influence their thinking. Setting those emotions aside to make decisions based on good information is one of the key responsibilities of any leader.

To do that you must remain focused on the key elements of a problem or a challenging situation. Consider how police investigate a crime. They want to know the facts: who, what, when where, why? By focusing on these key elements, they can establish and retain an objective perspective. An effective leader must also maintain objectivity. You will make better decisions if you focus on getting as much information as possible. Once you have sufficient information, you will often find that a solution is quite obvious.

Don't ignore other people's opinions in making decisions; just focus your efforts on establishing clarity. The truth is, as the leader, your team members are constantly looking to you for that clarity. Without it, they feel confused and uncertain. Since we all are victims of our own perceptions, clarity is a stabilizer. The clearer you are in your expectations and decisions the less confused and more certain your team members are about where your company is going.

Coaching

A leader should always be coaching the next generation. A strong leader is always preparing for his or her personal exit. The company must go on, and the best way to ensure that is to mentor the people who will follow you. If you fail to prepare, you prepare to fail.

Before you can mentor your successors, you must first fill your team with the right people. We have already addressed the issue of recruitment, so refer to that section if you need to do so. The critical point to be made here is that all the mentoring in the world will not turn a mare into a stallion or vice versa. So hire well!

How many times have you seen a company hire the wrong person just because a position needed to be filled? It happens, yet it is one of the worst things you can do to your company. Be tough when it comes to hiring well. Insist on getting the best person you can, and match his or her attributes and skills to the position being filled. Do not lower your standards just to get a position filled. That will just lower the performance of your entire team.

Once you have filled your team with the right people, it is your responsibility to prepare them for leadership positions with increasing responsibilities. Mentoring them takes time and effort. You need a plan for each individual, with an implementation schedule to keep you on track.

Share your experiences and your challenges with your mentees. Ask them for input, and give them careful feedback based on their comments. Point out other alternatives and why these alternatives may yield more desirable results. Be open in sharing the mistakes you have made, and what you have learned from those mistakes. As time progresses, give them more responsibility to make tough decisions. They must get used to making tough calls and being responsible for the outcomes.

Let them fail. Then help them recover from the failure. Anyone can read about failures in a textbook, but it is not the same thing as experiencing it firsthand. You can't teach a kid to hit a baseball by reading about it. Experience is a great teacher.

Remember, coaching is about imparting knowledge and then using that imparted knowledge to help your team members grow. Encourage and educate.

Perspective
Do all that you can to avoid living in "management land." I remember watching a television interview with Ross Perot, the founder of Electronic Data Systems and twice a candidate for the US presidency. In that interview, he stated that it is critical for an effective leader to get off the top floor and go down to the shop floor. This is how you stay in touch with your people. You learn firsthand the challenges they face as well as their aspirations.

You can't manage people from an ivory tower. No one likes that, and they certainly do not respect that management style. You manage your team by building strong relationships within the team. That is accomplished by staying in touch with them. Get out of your office and see what is happening.

I make it a point to do connect with my employees every day. Remember, you are not interrogating people, you are having conversations with them. Employees always check out of your company emotionally long before they walk out the door. Know your people. It always benefits the company.

Responsibility

Everything that happens to a company or within a company is the responsibility of the leader. Effective leaders embrace this responsibility. Weak leaders try to make excuses or to place the blame for poor performance somewhere else.

Your employees will naturally feel some level of responsibility for company performance, and you certainly want to foster that feeling. However, the willingness of your fellow team members to take responsibility does not in any way lessen the fact that the leader is ultimately responsible for everything that happens, good or bad. Until you are willing to accept this responsibility, you will not be in a strong position to accomplish your goals. People want to follow a strong leader. A strong leader accepts ultimate responsibility. It is as simple as that!

Taking responsibility does not mean taking credit. It is an interesting paradox, but it is one I believe in very strongly. If you truly want to be an effective leader, then you must accept the blame but deflect all of the credit. I know many people find this hard to accept. I have met many managers who felt that if they had to accept the blame for failure, they should take all the credit for success. I couldn't disagree more.

Credit and blame are not different sides of the same coin. Responsibility simply comes with the leadership position. It is part of the deal. Taking credit for success does not help you grow as a leader. I could argue that taking credit for success will hinder that growth. You probably do not deserve the credit anyway. Chances are any credit due most likely needs to go to someone else. Taking credit for your team's performance is a sure way to sow the seeds of discontent. Also, what could you possibly gain that furthers the goals of the company by accepting accolades? So, be quick to deflect any credit to others. People will appreciate the recognition, and that will help the company many times over.

This is not to say that recognition of the success of others does not need to be credible. It must be credible, or it will undermine your position as a leader. It is most often a case of simply recognizing something out of the ordinary. "Thank you" and "Atta boy" work very well. If your employee truly did something extraordinary, perhaps more recognition is in order. Use your own judgment. The bottom line here is, take all of the blame, but none of the credit!

Ultimately, an effective leader must have integrity. Integrity is earned each and every day. It is the combination of taking responsibility, bringing clarity, keeping your perspective, providing vision, and mentoring the next generation. It is your most precious attribute. Guard your integrity by continually analyzing yourself and making sure you are working toward strengthening your company.

Power and Authority

Let's briefly examine the difference between power and authority. In a previous chapter we discussed why it is important to grant people the authority needed to accomplish the tasks they have been assigned. Without granting them the necessary authority to accomplish a task, it is unrealistic to expect them to be responsible for the achievement of the task. So, I trust we all understand authority. It is equally important to understand that power and authority are not the same. Let's look at the differences and why those differences are important in leadership.

First and foremost, authority is granted; power is earned. The granting of authority normally comes with the assumption of a position or a title in an organization. Think of a judge in a court or an umpire on a baseball field. In both cases their authority over other people comes from assuming a position— judge or umpire. The position also comes with a certain amount of authority to make decisions on behalf of the organization that granted them that authority.

It then follows that authority itself has inherent limitations, in being able to accomplish the goals of an organization. An individual who has been granted authority can only be as influential in the accomplishing organizational goals as the amount or type of authority granted to him allows him to be. A baseball umpire can call you out but cannot send you to jail. So there are limitations on authority—limitations that are necessary and proper.

It should be noted here that I am talking about the normal exercise of authority granted in an organization. That does not mean that people do not overstep their authority, because that happens frequently. We often see instances in governmental organizations where individuals are actively pursuing their personal agenda and using the authority of their position as a means to do so. Therefore, the granting of authority within an organization is best done only to the extent necessary to allow the individual to accomplish that for which he or she is being held responsible. Grant authority, but do so with prudence and caution.

Power, in contrast to granted authority, is earned. Power is the ability to influence people and thereby influence situations. While authority is limited by the granting entity, power is virtually unlimited in its scope and scale.

Without getting overly involved in the psychology of power, it is interesting to note that people actually like giving power to others. There are many who believe that the giving of power is the natural way of things. I certainly don't know whether or not that is true. What I do know is that people will give you power once they are sure that you have earned it. I believe this is related to the fact that most people are more comfortable being followers than being leaders.

In any organization, whether it has a hierarchical or flatline structure, there is power. The people with power are the people who are listened to, respected, and have demonstrated an ability to accomplish necessary tasks. They are often people who prefer to work behind the scenes where they are the most comfortable and where they can do the most good for their organization.

There is nothing that says you must strive to acquire power. However, you will be a much more effective leader if you are also a powerful person, at least within your company. Any company will run more efficiently with people who can influence others to strive harder and achieve more. Anyone would rather work toward a mutually agreed upon objective (this is influence at play) rather than execute a task he has been authoritatively assigned.

So, how do you become a person who has some degree of power within your company? I doubt that there is only one way, but here are some guidelines:

- Be a good communicator. Tell people what they need to know, and do so with the intent of improving their situations.
- Be honest and frank. Don't be afraid to deliver bad news, so long as you do not point fingers. If your company is doing well, then tell everyone that. If you are struggling, tell them that too, so you can openly discuss ways to improve.
- Don't give orders. No one likes that. Ask people if they can help and show them respect by allowing them to say no. By asking people to help, you are giving them the opportunity to prove their worth without insisting they must do so. Leaders will accept the challenge.
- Hold your ego in check. If you need to show someone how important you are, then you can't be important. If you were, they would already know that.
- Respect the fact you need to deal with people as individuals, not as a collective. Everyone's situation is specific, and it is to your benefit to deal with each person as an individual.

I'm sure there are many more points to be made, but these are critical to becoming a person who uses power properly. It should be noted that is very easy to lose the power given to you. Once people stop trusting or respecting you, you lose your integrity and your power base. You may still have authority over others, but you have lost your ability to influence situations informally.

I place very little significance on authority, as it is very limited in its reach. Power is much more important, so long as that power is the ability to influence others. Cultivate your power base; use it properly and wisely. You will find you are a much more effective leader if you do this, and your company will achieve more because people will want to follow your lead.

Ways to Improve Your Leadership Skills

There are no born leaders. Leaders are developed, and the skills needed to be an effective leader are learned and honed over time. This is a never-ending process and one that presents many challenges. I think it helps to have a list of reminders (a checklist) to keep your leadership skills sharp. The checklist given here includes tips and questions that can help you continue to improve your leadership skills.

<u>Have a clear vision for yourself and for your team</u>. What do you want to accomplish as the team leader? Do you need to bring the team closer together so they function as a more cohesive unit? How can you educate your team to accomplish the goals you have set for them? Develop a vision for yourself that you can then communicate to others. Team members always look to the leader for direction, and you need to know what your vision is before you can effectively provide that direction. Start understanding your vision for yourself by asking these questions:

- What is your vision for yourself and your team?
- What do you want to contribute to others?
- How do you want to influence others?

<u>Know and utilize your strengths</u>. We all have strengths and weaknesses. Knowing what your strengths are and where they come from can enhance your ability to lead your team. Some people are great communicators; others are strong analysts, while others are consummate planners. These are just some examples of personal strengths.

Are your strengths derived from talents or skills? Talents are the abilities you are born with. Skills are the abilities you have developed over time. People can generally do much more with the talents they have than the skills they have developed, since talents are natural to them and skills are not. Knowing you are a good communicator tells you to use communication as a way to lead your team. Knowing you are a good planner tells you to use that skill as a way of showing your team how to achieve goals.

In these examples, both communication and planning are equally important, but knowing which one is your key strength helps you be a stronger leader. The basic questions to ask are:

- What unique talents were you born with?
- What skills have you developed over time?
- How can you use your talents and skills to influence your team members (show them the way)?

<u>Live in accordance with your morals and values</u>. You cannot separate your personal morals from your professional morals. Trying to do so is unsustainable. We all have morals and standards. The very same morals we live by in our personal lives must be carried forward to our professional lives. Otherwise, you will be constantly reassessing your difficult decisions, and that is an encumbrance to your team success.

A strong leader is consistent, and it is that consistency that others grow to depend on. Adjusting your standards to fit the situation confuses people, and they question whether or not they can trust and respect you. That is never desirable. So stick to your values, and act according to your own moral compass.

<u>Lead others with inclusiveness and passion</u>. It should be understood you cannot lead others unless they want you to be their leader. You can be their "boss" because that is an assigned position. However, to be their leader, you must win them over. One of the most important ways to do that is to make sure you are including them in decisions about issues that affect them. You always want them in the tent with you, not outside the tent looking in. A culture of inclusiveness is required to make that happen.

To be inclusive you must recognize the skills and talents of others. We all come to the table with certain capabilities. Recognizing those skills and utilizing them properly benefits both the individual and the company. Most people enjoy using their talents and skills, and that makes them happier team members. When you utilize people's talents, they will generally develop a passion for what they are doing. You want to harness this passion as it helps your team members become committed to the company's goal.

<u>Set definitive goals and implement concrete action plans</u>. Goal setting and effective planning are as critical to company success as anything you can do. The goals you set for your company must be both well thought-out and executable. To be achieved, a goal must have an understandable strategy and executable tactics. Tactics should be detailed and come with an associated cost. Remember, goals without strategies and tactics is just wishful thinking. Here are some critical points to remember about planning:

- A goal must be written, or it is just a thought.
- A goal must be understandable and measurable.
- All goals must have an executable timeline.
- Start by working backward from your desired endpoint.

Maintain a positive attitude. People naturally gravitate to positive leaders. Being a negative leader can work if you are in serious conflict, such as a war, but it is generally not a strong attribute of a company leader. If you are negative about the company's future, your team will pick up on that. The same is true about your attitude toward your competition. Negativity fosters a feeling of trepidation. Fear of the unknown can suppress productivity.

Conversely, leaders with a positive attitude foster a feeling of optimism. People naturally want to line up behind them and support their vision. Think of the number of social situations in which you have been involved where positive people seemed to act like a magnet, drawing others to them without even thinking about it. Use that to your advantage. It can be of great benefit to your company.

Improve your communication skills. We have spoken a great deal about the importance of communication with regard to effective leadership. I won't go over those points again. Just keep these ideas in mind as you strive to be a better communicator:

- Treat people as if they are all that matters. Give them all of your attention while you are actively communicating with them.
- Clearly communicate goals, vision, and expectations to others.
- Continually strive to improve your verbal and written skills.
- Do not forget the power of active listening. The better you listen, the better you communicate.

Admit mistakes. Since I have made more mistakes than I care to remember, I can honestly say that mistakes are the greatest teachers. We all have the opportunity to learn from our mistakes as well as from the mistakes of others. I have been fortunate to be able to attend college, as well as take advantage of numerous seminars and instructional courses. When I think about what was more valuable to me, college, seminars, instructional courses, or the mistakes I have made, I believe the mistakes have provided the greatest learning opportunities.

I am certainly not advocating intentionally trying to make mistakes. Most of us don't have to worry about that, since we make enough mistakes without trying. If you learn from them, then your mistakes have provided value to you and your company.

What I see as one downfall for many business leaders is the need to be the "Teflon man." That is, the person who refuses to admit his or her own mistakes to others. People see right through that, and it causes them to lose respect for you.

<u>Never stop learning</u>. Of all the things you can do to become a more effective leader, this is probably the easiest. Read, read, and read. Listen carefully, and avail yourself of as many learning opportunities as you can fit into your schedule. So long as you realize that you always have more to learn, you will be in good shape.

Conclusion

Leadership is a very complex topic, which is the reason numerous books have been written on the subject. If you concentrate on the items we have discussed here, you can greatly improve your leadership abilities. I believe in a holistic approach to leadership: leadership is not focused on just one element. You can't be just a good financial analyst, or just a good marketing analyst. You must be able to incorporate all of the key elements of leadership outlined above. Your ability to project a vision and then get your company lined up behind that vision will ultimately determine your success.

Certainly one of the biggest challenges you will face in leading an organization is what is known as the "Stockdale Paradox," as described in Jim Collins's book *Good to Great*. The term gets its name from James Stockdale, a

US naval officer who spent eight years as a prisoner of war. During that time he saw many fellow soldiers who were unable to live through their captivity. Strangely enough, one of the reasons he gave for this is that so many captives viewed their situation with extreme optimism: they were constantly thinking they would be freed in a few months or by some particular date. As those dates passed and the soldiers were not freed, they would become very discouraged. Basically, they would often lose hope.

Stockdale realized that it is critical to both keep your ultimate goal in the forefront of your mind while going about your daily activities and still recognize the reality of your situation. Business is exactly the same. You must always keep your goal of continual improvement in mind and be constantly working on ways to realize that improvement. At the same time, you must face reality.

If you are in a weak competitive position, you must recognize that in order to implement plans to gain a competitive advantage. If your production quality or service quality is less than acceptable, you must admit that fact and then devise a plan for improvement. In this manner, you can always keep your eyes on the ultimate goal, while living in your current situation and executing according to your current reality. This is where tactical measures support your long-term goals.

Putting it all Together

The leader of an organization is responsible for taking all that he or she has learned regarding how to successfully build a business and implement that knowledge. Make no mistake about it; your goal is to be successful. You must build a business, whether new or existing, that can compete and prosper. So, let's look at how you can put your business knowledge into practice.

Misconceptions

There are a lot of misconceptions swirling around about basic business practices. Here are some of the most common.

<u>Going outside the company for leadership is rare</u>. While it may be preferable to promote from within, companies frequently search outside their current personnel to find the right leadership. If you can find the right person already in your organization, then by all means promote from within. However, do not hesitate to go outside if you do not already have the right person in your company.

<u>Compensation is not a key driver to success</u>. Understand that all leaders want to be well compensated. Maybe you can do that; maybe you cannot.

You must live within the realities of your financial position. However, you cannot get a home-run hitter on what you pay the batboy. To believe you can is to be naïve. Having said that, remember compensation must be tied to performance. Nothing else will work. There can be no entitlements, only pay for performance.

<u>Long-range strategies alone do not produce long-range results</u>. Solid long-range strategies most certainly do produce solid long-range results, if the accompanying tactics are implemented properly. (Remember that each strategy must be accompanied by a set of tactics that can be implemented.) Analyze, plan, and reevaluate. Keep focused on goals, which are supported by strategies, which are achieved through solid tactical implementation.

<u>It's not what you start doing; it's what you stop doing</u>. Both of these strategies should be considered. It is important to stop doing anything that is not producing the desired results. It is also important to instigate new well-planned strategies. I hate to hear someone say they are doing something because that is what they have always done. That gets you nowhere. But, if you do stop doing something, you should already have thought about what you are going to start doing in its place.

<u>Motivating people never works</u>. As I have said previously, I am not a big believer in external motivation as a means to achieve success. However, there are times when just a little push is all someone needs to rise to the next level. Usually that is in the form of congratulations for a job well done and encouragement to rise even further. Remember, leaders do not need motivation, they bring motivation to the table.

These are certainly not all of the misconceptions about business. However, I see these as the main misconceptions. Now let's look at some of the truths about successful businesses.

Truths

<u>Getting the right people trumps all else</u>. This is the most basic truth of all. There is simply nothing more important that you can do for the long-term success of your company than to hire the right people and make sure they are correctly positioned in your company. (Refer to the chapter "Effective Methods for Managing People" for a more detailed explanation of this topic.) In selecting employees, character trumps specific knowledge. You can impart knowledge; character comes with the person. Talent trumps skills. Again, you can teach the required skills, but you cannot teach talent. Talent comes with the person. Choose talent first.

<u>Being truthful about your situation is critical to success</u>. Your company may be successful, or it may be struggling. In any case, it is imperative that you face the brutal truth, especially if you are struggling. Facing the brutal truth does not mean giving up. It means analyzing your strengths and weaknesses and evaluating your competitive position. If you do poor quality work, admit it and then put together a plan to correct it. If you lack good customer-service skills, admit that and devise a plan to correct that also. Only by being truthful can you make a plan for success.

<u>Concentrate on effective systems, not bureaucracy</u>. I have yet to deal with any governmental entity that was efficient, but governmental entities sure are good at building bureaucracies. These bureaucracies morph into self-perpetuating organizations. They seem to exist only to further their own existence, instead of providing the services they were originally created to provide. Think of the license bureau, the IRS, the county collector, and so on. Bureaucracy kills efficiency. Therefore, concentrate on systems that are efficient and that help you avoid bureaucracy.

<u>Technology is a tool, not a goal</u>. Use technology to help your organization run more efficiently. That is what it is there for. Don't get so immersed in technological improvements that you lose sight of the fact that it is just

a tool. As the operator of a store, you may want to give customers a special price on something to reward them for the business they have done with you. If your IT system will not permit you to do that because it cannot scan coupons, then your technology is not working for you.

Technology must permit you to operate your company the way you want it to operate. If it hinders that goal, then replace it with something that will do what you need. Choose technology that supports your core concept. Ask yourself, "Does this technology support my core concept?"

If the answer is yes, apply it relentlessly.
If the answer is no, ignore it as it is irrelevant.

<u>Ambition for the company must always exceed personal ambition.</u> This may seem blatantly obvious, but my experience is that many business owners regularly put their own personal interests ahead of the best interests of their company. You can often see this in the amount of compensation the owner takes out of the company simply because he or she can. All too often this excess compensation causes cash-flow problems. I have had to make that point to business owners many times.

Personal ambition can also be seen in personnel decisions. How many times have you seen a person, possibly a family member, employed by the company and placed in the wrong position? That doesn't help the employee or the company. It can be tough to always strive to put the needs of the company before individual needs. It requires a willingness to make tough decisions and then stick by those decisions.

Understanding these business truths and misconceptions can help you immensely in implementing strategies that benefit your business or organization. Unwavering adherence to these truths and misconceptions is, by itself, a winning strategy. You will be tested, so expect it.

All of these truths and misconceptions are critical to supporting the core concept of your company. Let's look at what a core concept is and why it is critical to long-term success.

Core Concept

In his book *Good to Great*, Jim Collins talks about the importance of core ideology (core concept), and why it is critical to success. My experience is that companies that live their core concepts are much more successful than companies who simply operate for profit.

Think of your core concept as the reason, beyond making money, you are in business. Are you there to provide opportunity for women, as Mary Kay does? Do you want to be an innovator in personal electronics, as Apple is? Are you trying to provide the greatest variety of consumer product at the lowest cost, as Walmart does? As you can see, there are various core concepts, and every company needs to have one that they adhere to. These core concepts must be distinguished from profitability, since profitability is the result of effective implementation of a viable core concept.

To establish a viable core concept, you must ask yourself what it is that you excel in that has a marketplace and fits into the basic business of your company. Look at Mary Kay. Just selling cosmetics on a multilevel marketing framework was not enough for them. They wanted to provide unlimited opportunity for women in business. I don't know if their products are better than those of their competition. I do know that their people are passionate about the company, and that passion has translated into billions of dollars in sales.

Also, look at Apple. Originally it was a personal computer company, built by Steve Jobs, (and others) who was later forced out by his own board of directors. In his absence the company floundered, and he was asked to return. The story goes that he agreed to return only if he could take the company away from computers and focus on small personal electronic devices. The board was hesitant but eventually agreed. The first new product was the iPod, an electronic music player. It was an enormous success. Next he introduced the iPhone, an even bigger success. We all know the story from there. The point is that he adhered to his core concept of transforming Apple from a computer company to a personal-electronic-device-and-music company. Adherence worked.

Finally, look at Disney. Walt Disney wanted to build a recreational park where families could come and enjoy the Disney characters live. It was a tremendous investment at the time and a big gamble. However, Walt Disney believed that if he could "make people happy" when they came to his park, he would be successful. He wanted every visitor (he insisted they be called guests) to experience live Disney magic. It worked.

Here we have three examples of companies with different core concepts. One wanted to provide opportunity for women, one wanted to provide innovative personal electronics, and one wanted to make people happy. Each of them adhered to their concepts. Each was successful. There is not a single mention of making money in any of these concepts. Why? Because if there is a market for your product or service and your core concept centers on being the best at delivering what customers in that marketplace want, the money will come. Passionate adherence to the concept is what makes the difference.

In my consulting business, my core concept was to try as best as I could to help struggling business owners to understand the fundamentals of business. I reasoned that if I could help them understand why they were struggling and get them to implement sound policies and procedures, I could help them become successful. So I always concentrated on uncovering the mistakes they were making and explaining those mistakes to the owner. Then we devised plans to address their deficiencies. I was fortunate in that in all the years I was consulting, I never had a client go out of business. I stuck to my concept of analyzing and teaching, and as time went on I was more convinced than ever of the need for this approach. I believe my clients all improved after going through this process.

There are a few things you need to know in formulating your reason for being in business (your core concept). I always like to start with the basic question, "What can I be the best at that has a market?" To break this down, first look at the industry you are in or want to get into. Start by asking yourself these questions:

Why do I want to be in this business?
Is there an established need for my products or services?
Is that need currently being met at a high level?
What are the barriers to entry into the industry?

Then ask these additional questions:

Do I have the ability to address the need?
What will it take for me to excel in this business?
How can I be the provider of choice in the industry?

The first set of questions is designed to establish whether or not there is a market for the goods or services you are contemplating providing. Just because you have ten years of experience working for a roofing contractor does not mean it is a good idea to open your own roofing company. If the needs of the marketplace are already being met at a high level and there are already plenty of roofing contractors in your city, the barriers to entry may be too great to reasonably overcome. If you are already in business, you should not need to ask those questions, though it doesn't hurt.

The next set of questions concentrates on your ability to fulfill the needs of your prospective customers (your marketplace). It is important to be brutally honest with yourself in answering the second set of questions. That can be difficult to do, especially if you really want to get into a particular business. You may tend toward wishful thinking.

I want to differentiate between being wishful and being optimistic. They are not the same, even though they are often used as if they are interchangeable. If you are optimistic, you believe that you can be successful in a business if you have a solid plan and implement that plan effectively. I like that attitude. You must have it to be successful. Such optimism arises from your belief that once you have done a solid opportunity analysis, the difference between success and failure depends on execution.

I know there are always factors that you cannot control. That is part of business, as it is part of life. You should try to anticipate those factors in your analysis and business plan to give you alternatives to address those factors.

If you are wishful, you design a plan that depends to some degree on an uncontrollable event. For example, you think you want to open a gas station at a particular location. The reason you chose that location is because you have heard talk that the state highway department will put in a road that would route traffic, which currently does not go by that location, directly by the chosen location.

So you build the gas station, and the highway department decides not to build the road. Now you do not have enough traffic to support the business, and the business fails. What was your mistake? It was in a poorly designed business plan. Your plan was totally dependent on a future event that was controlled by someone else—the highway department building a road at some point in the future. The plan was not optimistic; it was wishful. It was completely dependent on the highway department building a road that currently did not exist.

One last word about your core concept and its daily implementation in your business: Any core concept is only as good as the strategies devised to support that concept and its implementation. We have spoken at length about strategic implementation in a previous chapter. It is critical that you only create strategies that fall within the core of your business.

Don't be swayed by the "latest and greatest" strategy espoused by some "expert." Not all strategies work to support all core concepts. They are not always universally applicable to all businesses. If your core concept is to sell high-end jewelry to an upscale clientele, then the Walmart strategy of buying bulk quantities of merchandise to keep prices down will not work for you. It will run directly against your reason for being in business.

Focus

Once you have identified your core concept and committed to adhering to it, you can then focus on a few concepts that can lead you to success. Here is a list of important items to consider:

> Understand your economic driver.
> Achieving success is a process, not an event.
> Ego is not a good substitute for a good plan.
> A sound strategy must be fully budgeted to succeed.
> Encourage open debate and free exchange of ideas.
> Don't waste time on a lost cause.
> Fully analyze your mistakes.
> Be relentless in asking questions.

<u>What is your economic driver, and why do we care?</u> If you are Walmart, your economic driver is foot traffic, plain and simple. The more people you can get into your stores the more you will sell.

If you are an upscale jewelry store your economic driver is the number of high-income individuals you can get into your store. So marketing demographics are important to you, and you should know how to determine the right demographics and target them.

Finally, if you own a roofing company, your economic driver is not the number of telephone calls you receive, as many roofing companies believe. It is actually the number of roofing estimates you do. Again, this is a qualifier to the larger number commonly used, which is foot traffic or phone calls.

So, you must understand your economic driver in order to put together an executable marketing plan. Take the time to make sure you fully understand what drives your business. If you are in the car-repair business and you are spending a great deal of time on making your accounting exact, you are not concentrating on your economic driver.

Remember that success is a process without end. It may seem a bit daunting, but you must view business as a process without end. Celebrate your small successes and analyze your missteps, while at the same time understanding that no single victory or single mistake is the end. Sometimes it may feel like it when you have a setback, but with a good business plan and proper execution, you can go on. That is what counts.

Ego is counterproductive. This is a tough one to deal with on a daily basis. I have yet to meet a successful business owner who did not come with a high degree of self-assurance (myself included). You certainly want confidence and self-assurance. You need those qualities to get through tough times and to make hard choices. That is the reality. There will be hard choices to make, and self-assurance is important in helping you make them.

Ego is different. Ego causes you to make poor decisions by putting too much emphasis on individual abilities and too little emphasis on a solid, well-thought-out plan. Think of the number of times you have witnessed someone undertake a task you knew he or she was not ready for, either from lack of experience, lack of knowledge, or lack of ability. You knew it was not going to work, and maybe you even said so. If you can see the problem, why can't others see the problem? They are blinded by ego.

I want to emphasize that you want confident and self-assured people. They are critical to your success. However, you do not want to make decisions based on anything other than careful analysis and a detailed plan for success. The trick is to balance the two so that you do not lower anyone's confidence in themselves while at the same time being able to turn down proposals or ideas when it is appropriate and necessary to do so.

<u>A sound strategy is only sound if it is properly funded.</u> You can't implement a strategy to attract new customers or increase your business with current customers if you do not provide the funding to support the strategy.

Let's say you are suffering from inadequate customer service, and you have determined that one of the main reasons is not getting timely information to your customers. Further analysis shows that your customers are not happy because they cannot find out when their orders are going to be filled. (They just need to know when their orders are going to be shipped.) Before you can implement a fix for the problem, you first need to determine where the breakdown exists. Let's say it is inadequate information systems.

Therefore, you decide on a strategy of improving customer satisfaction by getting more timely information to your customers. What will that strategy entail? Do you need a new CRM (customer relationship management) system? Do you need updated internal information flow systems? Do you need broader access to existing information? To fix all of these problems you will have to invest in better information technology. That is never cheap! In this case, you cannot commit to resolving the problem without adequately funding improvements in your IT systems. If you can't or won't do that, then your strategy is doomed to failure.

Open discussion is a good thing. It seems to me that this is an obvious policy. Without it your view of your business is limited in scope. Without open discussion, everyone is walking around with blinders on, which narrows their field of view. I fail to understand how this can, in any way, benefit any organization.

I have learned so much simply from the free exchange of ideas. Not only does it give you access to broader perspectives, you also gain insight into people's thought processes. Both of these are very beneficial. Just remember that once a decision is made, everyone needs to line up behind that decision. They are more likely to do so if they have had input in making the decision.

Don't waste time on a losing proposition. This can be a tough one. Why? Because it is sometimes difficult to know when you are spending time and effort on a lost cause. Anyone can tell you that a "weekend duffer" is never going to win The Masters. It just is not going to happen. But most business issues are not that obvious. Most decisions contain at least some element of uncertainty.

What I am talking about here is when the likelihood of success is not zero, but it is extremely low. For example, Cardinal Health is one of the largest providers of hospital products in the United States. If you run a medical company specializing in home healthcare products in your community, can you successfully compete with Cardinal Health by expanding into the hospital market? Well, if your definition of success is that you occasionally sell something to your local hospital, then the answer is yes. However, if you seriously intend to compete with Cardinal Health on the broad spectrum of their hospital business, then that is a lost cause. Similarly, the owner of a small clothing boutique is never going to effectively compete with Walmart. So the small clothing boutique should stay out of the general merchandise business. But, such a business could be very successful selling designer clothing to upscale clientele, something that Walmart cannot do well.

The assignment of personnel can also be a great time waster and, by extension, a lost cause. We have all seen instances where employees have been assigned to duties they were not capable of doing, whether because they lacked knowledge or lacked aptitude. The good manager must be able to recognize these situations and make the needed corrections. It is not fair to either the company or the employee to let these problems persist.

These are just a few examples of wasting time on losing propositions.

<u>Learn from mistakes—we all make them</u>. I know this is just common sense, but I'm continually surprised by the lack of willingness to acknowledge when mistakes have been made. You see this all the time in companies who have poor customer service. They seem to spend an inordinate amount of time deflecting the cause of the mistake from their company. I really can't think of anything that makes customers angrier than when a mistake is made and the company goes into defense mode. Generally, the customer only wants a friendly voice and someone who will listen and help resolve the problem.

Learning from your mistakes is even more important than acknowledging them. Learning from mistakes does not mean blaming someone. If you have a good team, blame is irrelevant. What is relevant is identifying how the problem can be corrected and hopefully then improving your overall company performance.

For example, if you are in the home-repair business and you miss a scheduled appointment, your response should be twofold. First, apologize to your customer for the error and make some gesture of recompense for the mistake. Your apology must not only sound real; it must actually be real. You should value your customers so that when something goes wrong (as it will), you truly regret the mistake. Without that, you are doomed. Next, you must take the time to ask yourself what happened and how it happened. Just apologizing without taking some kind of corrective measure gets you nowhere.

Since mistakes are an everyday occurrence, we all have numerous opportunities to learn from them. The question is, "Am I willing to let this mistake teach me something that I can use to improve my business?"

<u>In business, it is very difficult to ask too many questions.</u> Not only is there no open discussion, but there are frequently no questions being asked at all.

In fostering an environment of free discussion, allowing open questions is paramount. We have all heard the statement that the only stupid question is the question that was never asked. As trite as that statement may seem, it is true. The challenge is to get the questioning going. Once you do get the questions flowing, it is very easy to maintain.

I like to start this process by asking a lot of questions that have no negative implications, such as, "How is that done?" or, "Can you explain that to me, because I don't really understand it?" Any line of questioning where the recipients do not feel threatened by the questions being asked will move the process forward.

For this to work there can be no forbidden questions, except those that are socially inappropriate or that deal with private information. You can't exert executive privilege and refuse to answer a valid question. If you share, your team will feel comfortable sharing also. When you are trying to make a difficult decision, at some point the questions must stop, and a decision must be made. Just don't be too eager to cut off that process. Questions are good and will pay big dividends in the long run.

One statement that I find very helpful is, "He who worries about what the boss will think is doomed!" That is certainly a little on the wishful side, since I think that most everyone cares about his or her supervisor's perception. So to say it doesn't matter at all is simply unrealistic. What does matter is that your team knows they can openly ask questions without fear of retribution. You must make that clear if you want a culture in which employees can ask questions for the betterment of the company.

Entrepreneurship

I hear this word used time and time again. Everyone has his or her own concept of what it is to be entrepreneurial. *Merriam-Webster* defines an entrepreneur as "a person who starts a business and is willing to risk loss in order to make money." This seems like a reasonable definition to me. However, what is critical to note is the risk-taking part of the definition.

Entrepreneurs take risks. But some take the risk with their own money, while others are only willing to risk someone else's money. I have found a profound difference between those who are willing to risk their own future and those who only want to risk someone else's future. That difference lies in the commitment to succeed. If you risk your own future, you are much less willing to walk away during difficult times. It is the difference between playing poker with your money and playing with house money. The level of commitment is just not the same.

Being willing to take risks is only one aspect of entrepreneurship. You must also create an entrepreneurial culture, a culture that values customers above systems, that values innovation above status quo, and that encourages input from anyone with something to add to the conversation. At the same time, the culture must stress that people are responsible for the results of their own actions and decisions.

Unfortunately, we have become a culture of Teflon people, and that is what we are teaching our children. The concept of responsibility is being abandoned and replaced by a culture in which no one is held responsible for the results of his or her actions. Sheltering children and adolescents from the consequences of their actions teaches them that no one is going to really hold them responsible for what they do. That just will not work in the business world. In business you are always held accountable for results and actions. Livelihoods and futures are affected by decisions and actions.

While it is unproductive to fixate on blame, as that gets you nowhere, it is critical to make sure you establish a culture of responsibility for actions and decisions. It is a matter of correcting mistakes and missteps so that you can continue to improve. If there is no responsibility, there is no real incentive to improve. So, don't fixate on blame, but do fixate on a culture of responsibility that provides continuous improvement.

How do you create a culture of responsibility? By making sure your employees are self-disciplined. This is one of the attributes to look for in the hiring process: is the candidate you are considering someone who feels responsibility for his or her actions and is that candidate disciplined in his or her thoughts and actions? If you cannot answer this question in the affirmative, don't hire that person.

You can't create an entrepreneurial culture of disciplined thought and actions with people who do not already possess that quality. An army imposes discipline on its soldiers through a strict military code. A business does not function efficiently if discipline must always be imposed on employees. That is an extreme waste of managerial time. So, surround yourself with self-disciplined people. Anything less is a compromise that you will come to regret.

We all know that bureaucracy is counterproductive. All levels of government have clearly shown us that. However, bureaucracy is created as a direct response to not having responsible people. A strong way to create disciplined and responsible people, and eliminate bureaucracy, is to encourage freedom of thought and open expression of ideas.

If you are encouraged to bring new ideas, then you will naturally take ownership of those ideas and the actions that result from them. In other words, you will have real skin in the game. Having skin in the game is a powerful incentive to succeed. People clearly understand this concept. However, they will not feel like they have any skin in the game if they are not encouraged to bring new ideas to the table. So, in that way the culture of free thought directly eliminates the need for an imposed bureaucracy. Think about it.

It is very important to be happy, but never be satisfied. You can enjoy your career, and you should, without ever feeling you have actually arrived at a pinnacle. To create a healthy culture, you need to be "happy but not satisfied." A healthy culture is one where everyone truly enjoys coming to work. Encourage that atmosphere by setting the right tone. Take an interest in the lives of your team members and take the time to let them know you are interested. That is an enjoyable environment.

Finally, it never helps to take a shotgun to a marksmanship competition. Change in an organization should be evolutionary, not revolutionary. Don't be in such a hurry to make changes that all you meet is resistance. Keep everyone in the tent by communicating well and taking a steady and methodical approach to improvement. Is this approach one of evolution or revolution?

There is a simple equation I heard somewhere that really helps explain the difference between revolution and evolution. Here it is:

$$\text{Short-term actions multiplied by time} = \text{long-term accomplishments}$$

So there it is. You didn't gain thirty pounds in one day, and you can't lose thirty pounds in one day. A great salesman is not the person who reads all the self-help books and dreams of success. A great salesperson is the person who makes ten sales calls a day, every day, day after day. Looking at success in this way you can see that long-term success is built on a never-ending series of short-term actions, or baby steps. Think long-term. Remember, it truly is evolution, not revolution!

   Good luck!

Index

Acid test 11, 21, 22
ADPO 12, 32
ADRO 12, 14, 27, 32
Asset 9, 11, 12, 14, 17, 18, 19, 20, 21, 22, 23, 24, 27, 28, 35, 37, 39, 48, 49, 118

Balance Sheet 9, 10, 17, 18, 19, 20, 21, 26, 27, 56, 64
Bonuses 2, 116, 121, 129, 130, 131
Break-even point 12, 14, 15
Budgeting 63, 64, 65, 66, 68, 69, 71

Cash flow 3, 14, 23, 27, 29, 30, 31
Closed Corporation 7
Collection letter 42, 43, 44, 45
Collection methods 3, 39
Commercial Property 48
Compensation 2, 17, 48, 19, 116, 120, 129, 130, 131, 136, 189, 190, 192
Competition 55, 73, 77, 85, 86, 88, 91, 92, 93, 94, 185, 193, 205

Cost of Goods Sold 10, 13, 15, 24, 25
Credit 2, 9, 10, 22, 24, 27, 36, 52, 112
Crime Policy 49
Current ratio 11, 21, 22, 35
Customer analysis 83
Customer-Centric 4, 107

Debit 9
Debt Ratios 12
Debt to assets 12
Debt to equity 12
Delegation 1, 154, 166, 167
Directors and Officers 47
documentation 133, 134

employment law 134
Employment Practices 48
Empowerment 162, 163
Entrepreneurship 203
Expenses 9, 10, 13, 15, 16, 17, 24, 25, 26, 31, 32, 35, 63, 64, 65,67 ,71, 74, 78

Financial Management 20, 54, 56

Goal Setting 56, 57, 58, 184
Gross Margin 3, 10, 12, 13, 14, 15, 24, 25, 26, 53, 71, 73, 74, 77, 78, 79, 89

Health Care 48

Income Statement 9, 13, 14, 15, 16, 19, 20, 24, 26, 27, 56, 68
Insurance 10, 13, 25, 35, 47, 48, 49, 50, 67, 68, 75, 116, 136
Interviewing 117, 118

Labor to sales percentage 11
Leadership 146, 153, 154, 156, 158, 159, 160, 162, 163, 168, 175, 176, 178, 179, 182, 185, 186, 189
Leverage Ratio 21, 24, 26
Liability 5, 7, 8, 9, 10, 22, 47, 48, 49
Limited Liability Company 8
Liquidity Measures 11, 21, 23

Margin Percentage 10, 14, 67, 89
Marketing 4, 29, 54, 55, 75, 76, 79, 81, 82, 83, 84, 89, 90, 91, 92, 95, 96, 100, 101, 102, 107, 109, 110, 111, 114, 137, 158, 186, 193, 198
Mary Barra 111
Media advertising 96
Money Myths 5, 6

Net Profit Percentage 25, 26
Networking 95, 96, 111

Partnership 7, 8
Performance reviews 120, 133
press releases 99
pricing policy 73, 77, 88, 89
pricing structure 55, 79, 85, 86, 87
Profit and Loss Statement 9, 10, 13, 54, 67
Profitability 1, 10, 11, 12, 14, 20, 24, 29, 30, 33, 63, 65, 67, 78, 89, 112, 116, 193
Promotion 89, 90, 91, 97, 107

Quick ratio 11, 21, 22

Recruiting 154, 155
Resistance 151, 163, 164, 165, 205
Respect 86, 108, 139, 140, 143, 144, 159, 160, 161, 164, 177, 181, 184, 186
Return on assets 11, 27
Return on equity 11
Return on Investment 28
Return on sales 11, 25
Revenue 5, 9, 10, 11, 12, 13, 14, 15, 16, 25, 26, 27, 29, 32, 55, 63, 64, 65, 66, 67, 68, 69, 71, 73, 75, 76, 77, 78, 79, 84, 85, 87, 89, 91, 93, 110, 111, 113

Sales forecasting 73, 74, 75, 76, 79, 101
Socratic method 160
Sole Proprietorship 7, 8

Subchapter S Corporation 8
SWOT analysis 4, 94, 100, 103

Threats 4, 55, 92, 93, 94, 104, 143
Time Management 148, 154, 168, 169, 171, 172, 173

Umbrella policy 49

Variable expenses 31, 67, 74

Walmart 77, 81, 87, 193, 197, 200
Workers Compensation 49
Working Capital 21, 23, 26, 35, 36, 37, 38, 74

www.ingramcontent.com/pod-product-compliance
Lightning Source LLC
Chambersburg PA
CBHW051642170526
45167CB00001B/290